Hands-On Automation Testing with Java for Beginners

Build automation testing frameworks from scratch with Java

Rahul Shetty

BIRMINGHAM - MUMBAI

Hands-On Automation Testing with Java for Beginners

Copyright © 2018 Packt Publishing

Commissioning Editor: Pavan Ramchandani
Acquisition Editor: Shriram Shekhar
Content Development Editor: Zeeyan Pinheiro
Technical Editor: Romy Dias
Copy Editor: Safis Editing
Project Coordinator: Vaidehi Sawant
Proofreader: Safis Editing
Indexer: Rekha Nair
Graphics: Alishon Mendonsa
Production Coordinator: Aparna Bhagat

First published: September 2018

Production reference: 1280918

Published by Packt Publishing Ltd.
Livery Place
35 Livery Street
Birmingham
B3 2PB, UK.

ISBN 978-1-78953-460-3

www.packtpub.com

`mapt.io`

Mapt is an online digital library that gives you full access to over 5,000 books and videos, as well as industry leading tools to help you plan your personal development and advance your career. For more information, please visit our website.

Why subscribe?

- Spend less time learning and more time coding with practical eBooks and Videos from over 4,000 industry professionals

- Improve your learning with Skill Plans built especially for you

- Get a free eBook or video every month

- Mapt is fully searchable

- Copy and paste, print, and bookmark content

Packt.com

Did you know that Packt offers eBook versions of every book published, with PDF and ePub files available? You can upgrade to the eBook version at `www.packt.com` and as a print book customer, you are entitled to a discount on the eBook copy. Get in touch with us at `customercare@packtpub.com` for more details.

At `www.packt.com`, you can also read a collection of free technical articles, sign up for a range of free newsletters, and receive exclusive discounts and offers on Packt books and eBooks.

Contributors

About the author

Rahul Shetty has worked with various CMM-level organizations and has managed the setting up of QA processes for projects.

Packt is searching for authors like you

If you're interested in becoming an author for Packt, please visit `authors.packtpub.com` and apply today. We have worked with thousands of developers and tech professionals, just like you, to help them share their insight with the global tech community. You can make a general application, apply for a specific hot topic that we are recruiting an author for, or submit your own idea.

Table of Contents

Preface

Java is one of the most commonly used software languages by programmers and developers. Are you from a non-technical background and looking to master Java for your automation needs? Then this book is for you.

This book is a guide that describes efficient techniques for effectively handling Java-related automation/projects. You will learn how to handle strings and their functions in Java. As we move, you will get to grips with classes, objects, and their usage. This book will help you understand the importance of inheritance and exceptions with practical examples.

By the end of this book, you will have gained a comprehensive knowledge of Java that will help you crack any job interview.

Who this book is for

This book is intended for software developers who want to step into the world of software quality assurance and perform automation testing using testing frameworks. This book assumes Java programming experience for writing tests.

What this book covers

Chapter 1, *First Programming Steps in Java*, will introduce Java to you, along with the steps for installation and writing a small program to get started.

Chapter 2, *Understanding Classes, Objects, and Their Usage in Java*, will cover the basic concepts, such as strings and variables, and how they are different from each other. We will also discuss objects and their importance.

Chapter 3, *Handling Strings and Their Functions in Java*, will show you how to define a string using the String class, using an example to demonstrate.

Chapter 4, *Building Blocks for Java Programs – Loops and Conditions*, will help you to understand important loops through examples.

Chapter 5, *Everything You Need to Know About Interfaces and Inheritance*, will cover some important concepts, such as interfaces, inheritance, function overloading, and function overriding.

Chapter 6, *Learning Everything about Arrays*, will cover one of the most important concepts in Java, arrays; we will look at a few examples to understand the working of arrays.

Chapter 7, *Understanding Date Class and Constructors in Java 11*, will dive into the Date class and constructors in detail.

Chapter 8, *Importance of the super and this Keywords and Exceptions in Java*, is all about two keywords: super and this. We will pick examples and explain how they are put to use in various situations while writing our Java code.

Chapter 9, *Understanding the Collections Framework*, will dive deep into the collections framework, which consists of interfaces and classes. We will have a look at the three major collections: List, Set, and Map. In addition, ArrayList from the List collection, HashSet from the Set collection, and HashMap and HashTable from the Map collection, will be discussed in this chapter.

Chapter 10, *The Importance of the final Keyword, Packages, and Modifiers*, will cover some important concepts, including the final keyword and importance of packages and modifiers in Java.

To get the most out of this book

Any prior knowledge of Java would be helpful during the course of the book.

Download the example code files

You can download the example code files for this book from your account at www.packt.com. If you purchased this book elsewhere, you can visit www.packt.com/support and register to have the files emailed directly to you.

You can download the code files by following these steps:

1. Log in or register at www.packt.com.
2. Select the **SUPPORT** tab.
3. Click on **Code Downloads & Errata**.
4. Enter the name of the book in the **Search** box and follow the onscreen instructions.

Once the file is downloaded, please make sure that you unzip or extract the folder using the latest version of:

- WinRAR/7-Zip for Windows
- Zipeg/iZip/UnRarX for Mac
- 7-Zip/PeaZip for Linux

The code bundle for the book is also hosted on GitHub at `https://github.com/PacktPublishing/Hands-On-Automation-Testing-with-Java-for-Beginners`. In case there's an update to the code, it will be updated on the existing GitHub repository.

We also have other code bundles from our rich catalog of books and videos available at `https://github.com/PacktPublishing/`. Check them out!

Conventions used

There are a number of text conventions used throughout this book.

`CodeInText`: Indicates code words in text, database table names, folder names, filenames, file extensions, pathnames, dummy URLs, user input, and Twitter handles. Here is an example: "To check whether Java is installed in our machine, navigate to `C:\Program Files`."

A block of code is set as follows:

```
package coreJava;
public class finaldemo {
        public static void main(String[] args) {
            //TODO Auto-generated method stub
```

When we wish to draw your attention to a particular part of a code block, the relevant lines or items are set in bold:

```
protected void abc() {
    //TODO Auto-generated method stub
  System.out.println("Hello");
}
```

Any command-line input or output is written as follows:

```
$ import package.classname
```

Bold: Indicates a new term, an important word, or words that you see onscreen. For example, words in menus or dialog boxes appear in the text like this. Here is an example: "Keep clicking on **Next** so that Java is successfully configured in our machine."

Warnings or important notes appear like this.

 Tips and tricks appear like this.

Get in touch

Feedback from our readers is always welcome.

General feedback: If you have questions about any aspect of this book, mention the book title in the subject of your message and email us at customercare@packtpub.com.

Errata: Although we have taken every care to ensure the accuracy of our content, mistakes do happen. If you have found a mistake in this book, we would be grateful if you would report this to us. Please visit www.packt.com/submit-errata, selecting your book, clicking on the Errata Submission Form link, and entering the details.

Piracy: If you come across any illegal copies of our works in any form on the internet, we would be grateful if you would provide us with the location address or website name. Please contact us at copyright@packt.com with a link to the material.

If you are interested in becoming an author: If there is a topic that you have expertise in and you are interested in either writing or contributing to a book, please visit authors.packtpub.com.

Reviews

Please leave a review. Once you have read and used this book, why not leave a review on the site that you purchased it from? Potential readers can then see and use your unbiased opinion to make purchase decisions, we at Packt can understand what you think about our products, and our authors can see your feedback on their book. Thank you!

For more information about Packt, please visit packt.com.

First Programming Steps in Java

1

Welcome to *Hands-On Automation Testing with Java for Beginners*. This is the only book you will find on the internet that teaches every topic needed to emerge as a strong Java automation tester. It contains easy teaching and simple techniques to effectively handle Java-related automation/projects. Considering that we will cover each and every topic of core Java, with detailed explanations, this will really help us develop and grade our own Java automation projects.

All the core Java concepts are explained from scratch. We do not assume that readers have any prerequisite knowledge, so we consider all readers to be from a non-coding background, and we teach each and also support them with examples that we will use in real time. Hence, we will not stick to only theories.

When you check for courses in the market, you should try to learn one new concept. You just see three lines of definition followed by examples; that's all. But here, we will understand why, when, and where we are using the **object-oriented programming systems** (**OOPS**) concept in Java. There will also be proper programming examples, showing a particular OOPS concept in real-time usage. In this way, our book will drive through real-time projects; it's all about practical learning. This will come into play when we start with Java collections, such as core Java, which is one of the main concepts in our book since it is definitely required for you to start your basics and to develop an automation framework in your workplace. Also, since Java collections is one of the core parts, throughout the entire book we will take utmost care in providing all the necessary practical scenarios for each Java collection that we will discuss.

We will be working on tricky Java programs, looking at printouts, prime numbers, Fibonacci series, and pyramids. We will sort out print in descending order, looking at array matrices, and printing the maximum column numbers. This book will provide you with detailed strategies and tips that you will need to use when approaching and designing a logic for these programs. This will help you to think beyond the boundaries and get the logic that you will need to write difficult Java programs.

Programs discussed in this book derive from commonly asked questions during interviews in many companies. You will receive help with those questions, with detailed solutions, and the methodology to approach that logic. So, this book is mainly focused on core Java. We are not dealing with swings and buttons, which are out of scope for Java learning in this book.

In this book, we will be learning core Java, collections, and other concepts such as loops, classes, and arrays . These are more than enough for you to start and develop a Java project. Whichever field you are put in, the knowledge gained from this book will help you start testing in the automation projects right away.

This chapter will cover the following concepts:

- An introduction to Java and its installation
- Working with the Java editor tools
- Writing your first executable program in Java

An introduction to Java and its installation

The first thing that comes to mind when we speak about Java is that it is platform-independent. This feature has made Java a hot programming tool in the market. So what exactly does platform-independent mean?

The code that we write is independent of the environment; be it Windows, Unix, Linux, or Solaris. Basically, when we write a Java program, the Java compiler converts the program to bytecode. When we run the Java code, the Java compiler converts the entire programming code to bytecode. For example, we are working on a Windows machine. When we run the program and the Java compiler runs and creates bytecode for us, this bytecode can be taken and executed on any other platform, such as Linux, macOS, and Unix. So this means we are developing a bytecode in Windows, and that bytecode is runnable on any other platform. So this is what we mean by platform-independent.

This is a really cool feature that we have in Java programming. Whenever you ask someone to download Java, the first question you will be asked is, is it JDK or JRE? People tend to get confused between these two terminologies. We need to be clear about this before we start downloading and configuring Java in our machines. Let's have a look at both JRE and JDK:

- **JRE** stands for **Java Runtime Environment**: It is responsible for running our Java program. If our aim is to just run a plain Java core code then JRE is sufficient.
- **JDK** stands for **Java Development Kit**: It is used to debug our Java code, or if we want to have the Java documents or something similar.

JDK contains JRE, Java documentation, and debugging tools, and other cool things. It's an entire Java kit from which we will get all of its components. So it's up to us what we download, but I would recommend we only have JDK to be on the safe side. If we want to just practice and run our program, JRE is also sufficient, but let's stick to JDK.

So now let's go back and download Java from the internet and try to configure it in our machines. To download Java, navigate to the following page: `https://java.com/en/download/`. When you click on the **Free Java Download** button, as shown in the following screenshot, the JRE version will be downloaded:

But we intend to use JDK for our program, so navigate to the following site: `https://www.oracle.com/technetwork/java/javase/downloads/index.html`. Here, there are multiple versions of JDK. The latest version out in the market right now is Java SE 10.0.2. Click on **DOWNLOAD**, as shown in the following screenshot, so that all the components are downloaded and configured in our machine:

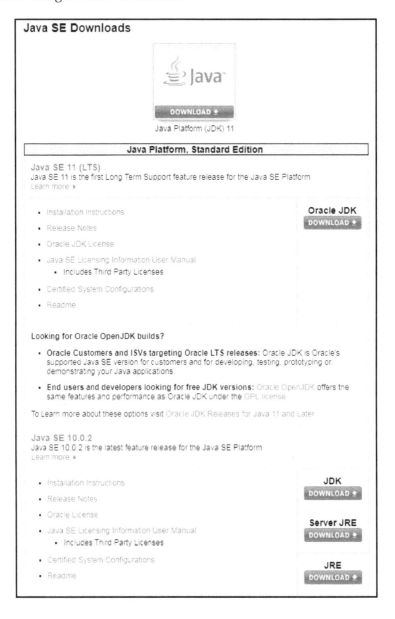

It takes a while because there are quite a few steps to configure it. Keep clicking on **Next** so that Java is successfully configured in our machine. To check whether Java is installed in our machine, navigate to `C:\Program Files`. If we find the folder named `Java` there, it means that Java has been successfully installed in our machine. The `Java` folder is shown in the following screenshot:

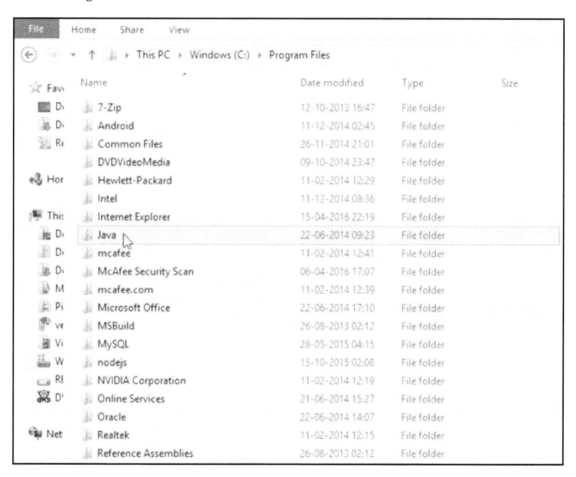

An important point to remember here is that if we are on 64-bit, only then will we see this `Java` folder in `Program Files`. If our machine is on 32-bit, then we need to go back to `Program Files (x86)` to get the `Java` folder.

We can check our system type by going to **Control Panel** and clicking on **System**. The system I am working on is 64-bit, as displayed in the following screenshot:

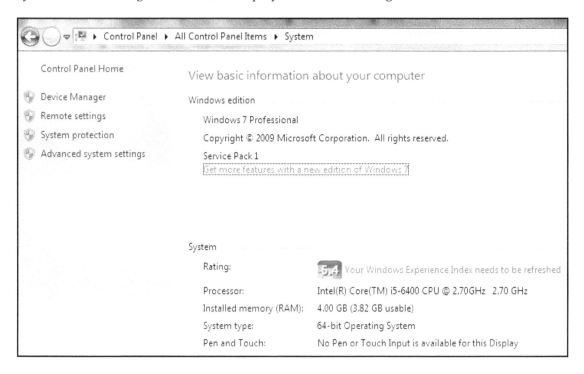

After it is successfully downloaded, we enter the `Java` folder and observe that both JDK and JRE have been downloaded. We enter the JDK folder and copy the entire file path. We are doing this because we need to set environment variables. Setting environment variables means that we are letting our system know where the Java folder is located.

In our case, the Java folder is in `C:/Program Files/Java/JDK`, but Windows doesn't know where exactly it is. So to make our system aware of the location, we will place the JDK home path in our system variables. This will help our machine know where the Java folder is located, so that whenever we run our program, it will identify the exact JDK version and run our program. To update this in system environment variables, we copy the entire JDK path. Go to **Control Panel**, select **System and Security**, select **System**, and click on **Advanced System Settings**. In **Advanced System Settings**, select **Environment Variables**. When we click on **Environment Variables**, the following window appears:

When we click on **New** in the **User variables for Rahul** section, we will get a prompt to add a **New User Variable**. We put in the name as JAVA_HOME, paste the JDK path in the variable value text box, and click on **OK**, as shown in the following screenshot:

This is how we let our system know where exactly the Java folder is present. We will need to update another variable too. To do that, we go back to the JDK folder and enter the bin folder. We will see multiple .exe files, as shown in the following screenshot:

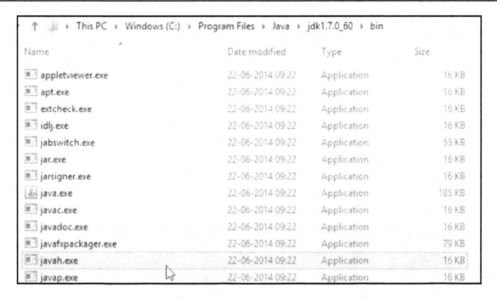

We copy the `bin` folder location path and return to our **System Properties** window. In **System Variables**, we will see a variable named `Path`. Double-clicking on it will show us a prompt to **Edit System Variable**, as shown in the following screenshot:

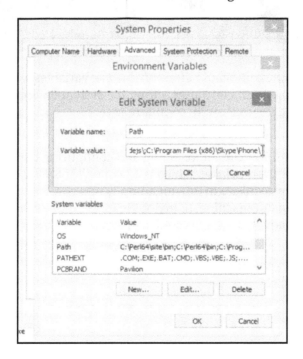

In the variable value, we go to the end, add a semicolon, and paste the `bin` folder path. This means we are setting the `Path` variable to the `bin` folder. We also create a new variable called `JAVA_HOME`, pointing to the `Java` folder. We need to set these two variables before we start working on Java. Once we set both the variables and click on **OK**, we will successfully set **Environment Variables**.

If we want to cross-check if the environment variables are properly configured or not, we use Command Prompt. In Command Prompt, we enter `java -version` and hit *Enter*. If we get an output as shown in the following screenshot, it means that Java has been successfully configured on our system:

```
C:\Windows\system32\cmd.exe                                          _  □  ✕

C:\>java -version
java version "1.7.0_60"
Java(TM) SE Runtime Environment (build 1.7.0_60-b19)
Java HotSpot(TM) 64-Bit Server VM (build 24.60-b09, mixed mode)

C:\>
```

 If we run the command before adding the variables, we will see that Java is not recognized. Only after setting the system environment variables will we be able to successfully configure Java.

The previous instructions take care of installing and configuring the system from our end. Next, we will try to download Eclipse, which is a Java editor tool where we write, run, and debug our code. As a pre-requisite to downloading Eclipse, we have to make sure that Java is properly configured in our machine. If any of the installation or configuration steps haven't been done correctly, Eclipse will not install properly.

Working with the Java editor tools

Here, we are going to look at the editor tool that we will be using to write our Java code. There are many tools available in the market that can act as a new Java editor, but I personally prefer using Eclipse. It comes with lot of in-built features and syntax additions. We will see other advantages of Eclipse as we progress. Some of the advantages cannot be discussed theoretically, so once we progress and start coding practically, we will understand how it prompts us to write a correct syntax. So, throughout the course of book, we will write all our Java code in the Eclipse IDE editor.

First, we download the Eclipse IDE editor and take a look at the interface that it has to offer. The following link will take us to the official website of Eclipse: `https://www.eclipse.org/downloads/`. The website will look like the one shown in the following screenshot:

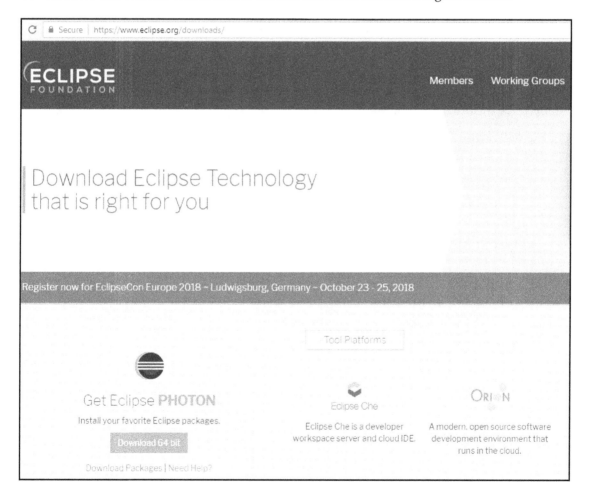

When we click on **Download Packages** below the **Download 64 bit** button, it takes us to the following page:

We will be using **Eclipse IDE for Java EE Developers**. We can select between 32-bit or 64-bit, depending on the system we are working on. We already know how to check if our system is 32-bit or 64-bit, by accessing **Control Panel** and following the instruction given during the installation stage.

An important thing we need to ensure is that our Java version is compatible with the IDE we are downloading. If our system is 32-bit and we download 64-bit Java, then Eclipse will not open. So ensure that our system, Java, and Eclipse versions are all on the same line.

The file will be downloaded in a ZIP folder form and we can extract it. The following screenshot shows folders that will be present in the `eclipse` folder:

If we double-click on the `eclipse.exe` file, the Eclipse UI will open.

If we want to write our Java code, we need to create a Java project. Right-click on the white pane window, which is on the left side, and click on **New** | **Project**. This is shown in the following screenshot:

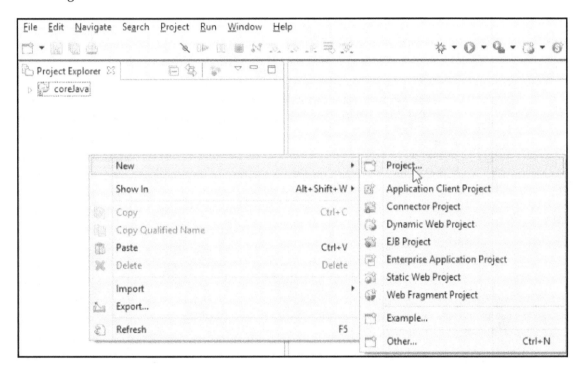

We get a prompt to tell to Eclipse what kind of project we are working on, as shown in the following screenshot:

As we can see, a lot of different frameworks are available, such as **Java Project**, **C/C++**, and **Android**, but we are interested only in the Java project, so we select **Java Project**, and click on **Next**. We will get a **New Java Project** window where we will fill in all the information for our new project, as shown in the following screenshot:

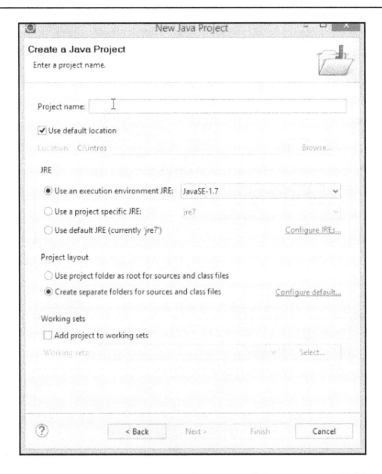

We select a project name for our Java project that we will be creating. We'll name our first project `coreJavaTraining`. Click on **Next** and then **Finish**. We will get a prompt asking us if we want to **Open Associated Perspective?**; select **No**:

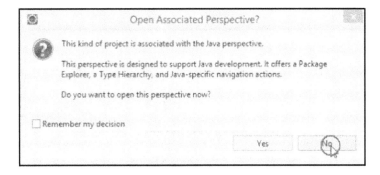

This will successfully create `coreJavaTraining`. Within the project, there is a source folder that is automatically created. This means we need to write our classes inside this source folder. What exactly are the classes? Basically, all Java code is written inside a class. When we write Java in Notepad, we open Notepad, write the Java code, and save that particular Notepad file with the `.java` extension. But in Eclipse, all that work is done by this tool itself. So all we need to do is create a class and that will give us a proper template. We right-click on the source (`src`) file and click on **New** | **Class**. We will get a **Java Class** prompt where we will be entering the class name. We will name this class `Firstclass` and ensure that we select the **public static void main (String[] args)** check box; we will discuss the importance of this later. And, finally, we click on **Finish**. This is shown in the following screenshot:

We see that the in-built hierarchy is already created for us, as Eclipse creates an outer template. We can see in the editor that a class and `public static void main` is present. All this is created by the Eclipse tool. If we were writing normally on Notepad without using any tool, we would need to create the template. But in Eclipse, all we need to do is give the class name. The code we will be typing will be encapsulated in the class; that is, inside the brackets of the class. Whatever name we use while creating the file will be the class name.

All the execution of the code will be placed in `public static void main` because whenever we run this file, Java control will go directly to this block. It will not touch any of the code written outside `public static void main`. In short, we write the code outside the `public static void main` block, but ultimately we need to call that code inside the block. This is because only the `main` block is responsible for the execution of our Java code. That is why we write `public static void main`. We will learn about the `public` and `void` keywords as we move further in this book because it is too early to get into the details of these now. We can see the template in the following screenshot:

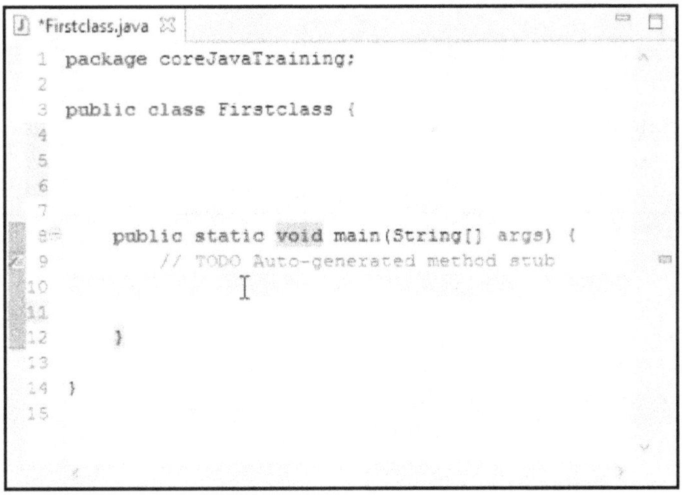

```
J *Firstclass.java ⊠

 1   package coreJavaTraining;
 2
 3   public class Firstclass {
 4
 5
 6
 7
 8       public static void main(String[] args) {
 9           // TODO Auto-generated method stub
10
11
12       }
13
14   }
15
```

The class created by the Eclipse tool

Writing your first executable program in Java

Let's start with our basic coding in this section. If we want to print something in our output, there is a command in Java called `System.out.println()`. This command will print the output in the console. Let's say we would like to print `hello world`, and when we run the following code, `hello world` will be printed in our output console:

```
Firstclass.java
```

So let's run the code. There are two methods to run the code:

- Right-click on the filename in the **Project Explorer**, click on **Run As**, and select **Java Application**.
- Or, we could click on the run icon given in the toolbar and click on **OK** on the **Save and Launch** window. The icon looks like this:

This will run our code and print our output. The following screenshot shows the `hello world` message on our editor:

```
package coreJavaTraining;

public class Firstclass {



    public static void main(String[] args) {
        // TODO Auto-generated method stub


        System.out.println("hello world");
    }

}
```

Markers Properties Servers Data Source Explorer Console Snippets
\<terminated> Firstclass [Java Application] C:\Program Files\Java\jre7\bin\javaw.exe (17-Apr-2016 6:06:27 pm)
hello world

Output displaying hello world as per the code

In short, `System.out.println()` is used to print in our console. We will be using this in almost all our examples for our demonstration of practical examples. If we remove `ln` from the statement, it will not print the output in the next line.

Let's try printing a statement that will display the output of two print commands on the same line. Here, we add a `System.out.println("hi")` statement before the `hello world` statement. If we run the code, the output will be as follows:

```
Firstclass.java

 1  package coreJavaTraining;
 2
 3  public class Firstclass {
 4
 5
 6
 7
 8      public static void main(String[] args) {
 9          // TODO Auto-generated method stub
10
11          System.out.println("hi");
12          System.out.println("hello world");
13          |
14      }
15
16  }
17
```

```
Markers  Properties  Servers  Data Source Explorer  Console  Snippets
<terminated> Firstclass [Java Application] C:\Program Files\Java\jre7\bin\javaw.exe (17-Apr-2016 6:07:13 pm)
hi
hello world
```

Output is displayed on two separate lines

Observe how `hi` is displayed on one line and then `hello world` is displayed on the next line. Here, `ln` displays the output in the next line. If we remove `ln` from both the statements and run the code, the message will be displayed as follows:

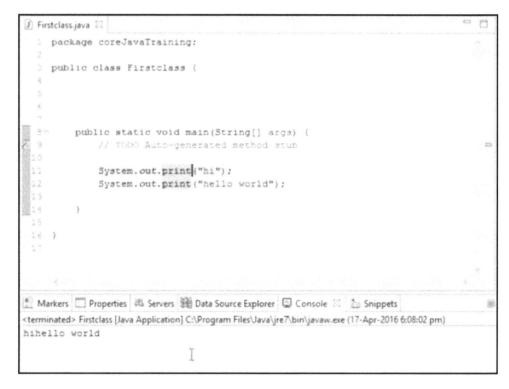

Output is displayed on the same lines

We see, `hihello world` printed on the same line.

If we write our code, and then we want to check the output partially, we don't need to remove the line of code; all we need to do is just comment it out. We can comment it out by simply putting double slashes (//) at the beginning so that Java will not pick the line. This is shown in the following screenshot:

Commenting using double slashes

If you remove the slashes and the statement is just some random words, then it will throw an error. We will see a red underlined code. This means there is an error at the line with a cross mark. This is shown in the following screenshot:

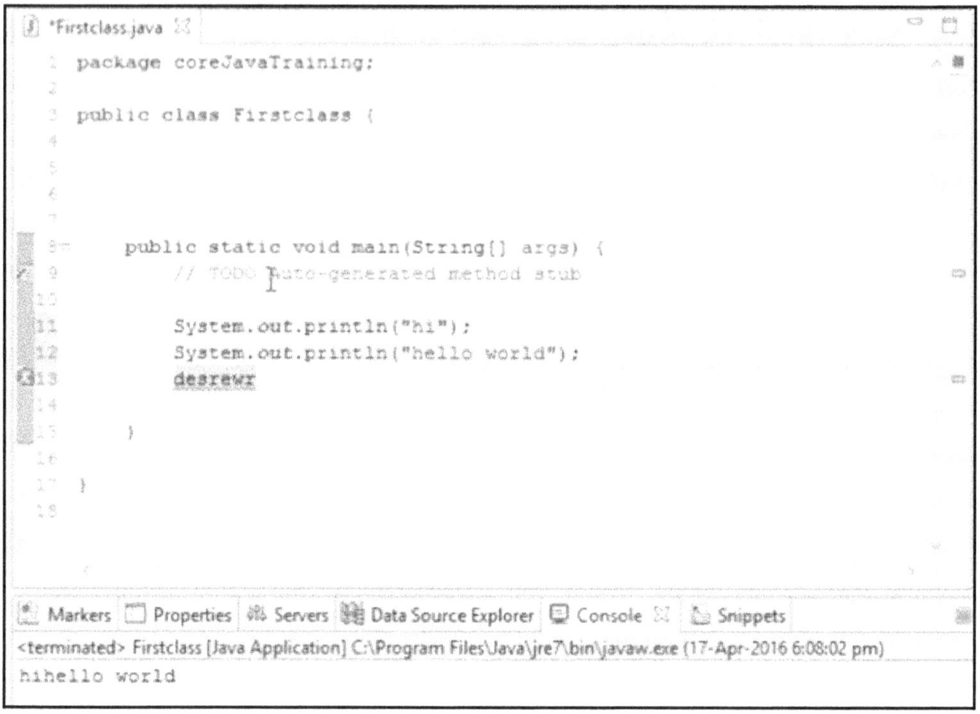

Error is flagged with a cross mark besides the line number

Add the backslashes again to comment out the error.

Remember, here we are writing our actual code in the `main` block only. What if we want to print an integer?

Let's say we want to print the number 4. To print it, we first need to store it in a variable and then we will print the variable. So when we print the variable, the value presenting that variable will be printed automatically. For this example, we pick the number 4, and we assign the number in a variable called a. The problem here is that a does not know what data type is being assigned to it. So, we have to explicitly mention that a is an integer. If we do not mention that a is an integer, it throws an error.

In short, we are first creating a variable called a which only acts an integer and then places an integer value 4 into this. The following screenshot illustrates the example we are talking about:

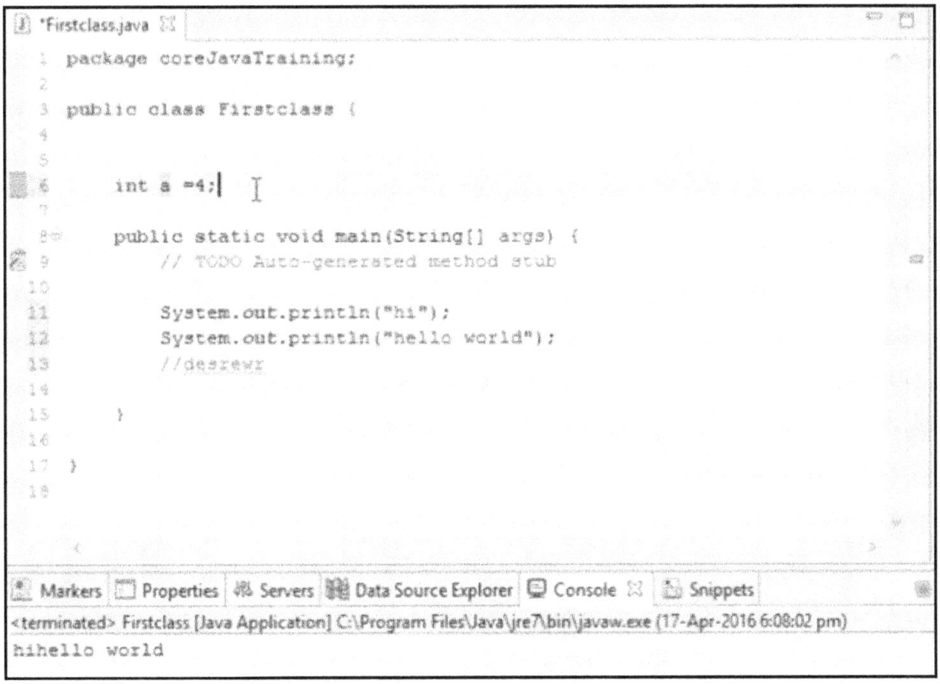

Value 4 is assigned to the variable a

So, with this type of code, we can type it outside, but if we want to print it, we will have to type it in the main block. In this example, we want to print the value of a so we add another `System.out.println(a)` statement. The editor will throw an error for the variable a in the `print` statement. To know what the error is, we hover our mouse over the error and a pop up is displayed showing the error with a possible fix, as shown in the following screenshot:

Error details is displayed when the mouse is hovered over it

There will be an option to click on in the error detail. This will automatically resolve the error by adding the required content. This is an amazing feature that the editor has and it is very helpful as we move onto more complex examples.

In our example, when we click on `Change 'a' to 'static'` in the error detail pop up, `static` is added to the variable `a` and we are able to run the code. On running the code, the console will look like this:

Output displaying the value of a as per code

We will be getting into the details of what exactly `static` is in the later chapters

Summary

In this chapter, we had a short introduction to Java. We then installed and configured the various tools required to work with Java. Moving ahead, we took a look at the editor we will be using to write our own Java code.

Finally, we executed our first example and saw how the editor works and how errors are handled by it.

In the next chapter, we will learn about some basic concepts, such as strings, variables and methods, and how are they different from each other using code.

2
Understanding Classes, Objects, and Their Usage in Java

In the previous chapter, we covered a short introduction to Java and how to install the editor that we will be typing our code in. We also wrote and executed our first code on the editor.

In this chapter, we will go deeper into some basic concepts, such as strings and variables, and how they are different from each other. We will also see what methods are and how they are put to use with different code. We will discuss why objects are important in our code and how we can implement them.

In this chapter, we will cover the following topics:

- Difference between strings and variables
- Using methods
- Importance of classes and objects in Java

Difference between strings and variables

In Chapter 1, *First Programming Steps in Java*, we printed a string and the variable. If we look closely, when we print a variable we are not using double quotes, but when we print a string, we are using them. This is because the value is already present in the variable, hence we need not use any double quotes. If we use them, Java considers it to be a string and the output will be printed as the letter a in the following example. If we run this and observe the output, the letter a will be printed as shown in the following screenshot:

```
Firstclass.java
 1  package coreJavaTraining;
 2
 3  public class Firstclass {
 4
 5
 6      static int a =4;
 7
 8
 9      public static void main(String[] args) {
10          // TODO Auto-generated method stub
11          System.out.println("a");
12          System.out.println("hi");
13          System.out.println("hello world");
14          //dasrewr
15
16      }
17
18  }
19
```

Markers Properties Servers Data Source Explorer Console Snippets

\<terminated\> Firstclass [Java Application] C:\Program Files\Java\jre7\bin\javaw.exe (17-Apr-2016 6:17:06 pm)

```
a
hi
hello world
```

Output displaying the value of a as per the code

If we don't use double quotes, Java will check whether there is any variable defined with this letter. If so, it prints the value present in that variable. If there is no variable defined, then it gives an error. If we comment out the variable declaration, what we see is an error. Hovering the mouse over the variable, we will get a prompt saying **Create a local variable 'a'**, or we can use it by adding double quotes:

Quick fixes drop down with suggestions to correct the code error

In short, if we simply use double quotes, the variable will be treated as a string, but if we don't use double quotes, we must declare the variable somewhere. That is the difference between printing out strings and printing out variables.

Using methods

Basically, methods are blocks in our Java class. Let's write one block here as an example, and observe where the opened and closed brackets are placed. The following example shows one complete block:

```
public void getData()
{
    static int a=4;
}
```

In this code, we have named the block of code `getData()` and `void` is the return type for this method.

If we are expecting to return a number from the method, and the number is an integer, then we have to write `integer` in place of `void`. The same applies with strings; if we are planning to return a string from the `getData()` method, then we have to declare it as a `string`. If we are not returning anything, that is, if we are simply writing a few lines of code, then we leave it as `void`.

Take a look at the following screenshot:

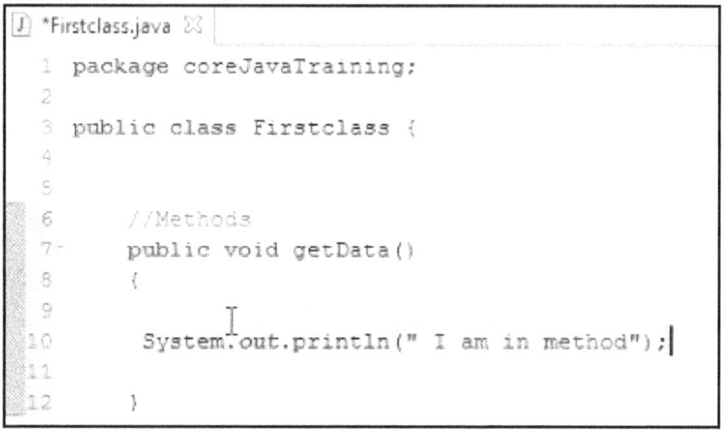

```
1  package coreJavaTraining;
2
3  public class Firstclass {
4
5
6      //Methods
7      public void getData()
8      {
9
10        System.out.println(" I am in method");
11
12     }
```

Return type is given as void for getData()

Here, we are not returning anything, so we keep it as `void`.

Let's add a `return 2;` line below `System.out.println(" I am in method");`. Here, we are returning a number that is an integer. That's why we will receive an error here. If we hover our mouse over the error shown over `return 2;`, you will see a suggestion, **Change method return type to 'int'**:

```
J *Firstclass.java ⅩⅩ

  1  package coreJavaTraining;
  2
  3  public class Firstclass {
  4
  5
  6      //Methods
  7      public void getData()
  8      {
  9
 10      System.out.println(" I am in method");
 11      return 2;
 12
 13      }            Void methods cannot return a value
 14
 15                   2 quick fixes available:
 16      public           Change method return type to 'int'
 17       //              Change to 'return'
 18       Sy.
 19      System.out.println("hi");
```

Quick fixes drop down with suggestions to correct the code error

On clicking on the suggestion, our IDE automatically modifies the return type to integer and the error disappears. The same is also the case with the string data type.

We will discuss the `public` access modifier later on in `Chapter 10`, *The Importance of the final Keyword, Packages, and Modifiers*. There is a lot to discuss since there are different access modifiers in Java, such as `public`, `private`, `protected`, and `default`. We will take a look at each access modifier with appropriate examples so that they are explained in detail. For now, let's just accept all access modifiers as `public`.

Now you must be wondering why these methods are present in Java. What is their use?

Let's say that we are executing a 10-line block of code, for example, to add two integers on a page. Now every time we reach a page that requires us to add two integers, we have to write the 10 lines of code again. Maybe replicating the 10 lines of code won't matter for one instance but what if we were to require this block of code for 10 instances throughout the entire project? So 10 pages and 10 lines of code makes 100 lines of code that we are replicating in a single Java program. So to avoid that, we write all the 10 lines of code into one block, and we name that block as, for example, `getData` or anything else. Thereafter, whenever we require the 10 lines of code that we typed, we can simply call the `getData` method. All the 10 lines of code will fall into that particular block, and it will get executed. In this case, we avoid writing the code 10 times; we write it only once in a method and call that method whenever it is required.

Let's explain this with an example:

```java
package coreJavaTraining;

public class Firstclass {

    public void getData()
    {
        System.out.println(" I am in method")
    }
    public static void main(String[] args) {
        System.out.println(a);
        System.out.println("hi");
        System.out.println("hello world");
    }
}
```

In the preceding class, we will consider " `I am in method`" as the 10 lines of code that we were talking about earlier. We want to call this method, but here the `getData()` block is outside the `main` block, which means that the code cannot be executed. To execute it, we must move it inside the `main` block. In most cases, people just copy the code inside the `main` block and then receive an error since no methods are allowed inside the `main` block. The method should be written outside the main block, but inside the class. If we write something outside the class, there is no point since Java does not catch it. But if we write the method outside the `main` block, how do we get it inside the `main` block? For that, we need to create an object for the class where our method is defined. Here, our methods are defined in the `Firstclass` class, so we create an object for this class and with that object we can access the methods and variables present in the class.

In the next section, we'll see what the objects are, where we use them, and how objects are used to call the methods and variables.

Importance of classes and objects in Java

Objects are instances or references of a class. So we can call the methods and variables present in this class with the help of their objects. We cannot call methods and objects directly, we can only use them with the help of their objects. So first, we need to create objects for the class, and then we can call the method inside the `main` class.

Let's take a look at the previous example to explain this:

```
package coreJavaTraining;

public class Firstclass {

    public void getData()
    {
        System.out.println(" I am in method");
    }
    public static void main(String[] args)
    {
        System.out.println("hi");
        System.out.println("hello world");
    }
}
```

Since the `main` block is already in the class, why do we need to create an object again for this class and call it?

The answer is that there is no way that the `main` block will come to know about the method outside it until and unless we create an object to call the method. There is an exception for that, which is the `static` variable, saying that the method is static. So, in general, accessing other methods is only possible with objects.

Creating an object in Java

First, we need to allocate some memory for the object in the class. Memory can be allocated with the help of the `new` operator followed by the class name. Then we define an object name for it. The return type should always be the class name. This is the syntax for creating a memory allocation for a class. So the code for memory allocation for the preceding example will look something like the following:

```
Firstclass fn=new Firstclass();
```

Here, we say `fn` is the object of the `Firstclass` class. Now that we have created an object, let's see how we can access it.

Accessing an object in Java

To access the method of the class, we write the object name and then . (dot). All the methods that qualify for the class are displayed in a drop-down—this is another great feature in Eclipse. We can just look for the method in the drop-down rather than searching for it through the code.

In the example, we are using the getData() method. The rest of the methods shown are all built-in Java methods. Observe how the methods are displayed:

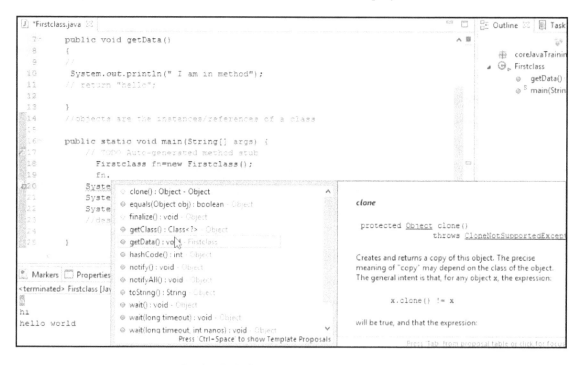

Drop-down showing all the class methods available to the editor to use

On clicking on getData(), the getData() block will be transferred to the line where the object was called, and when we run the program, the code will be executed as it is part of the main block. The accessing code will finally look like this:

```
fn.getData();
```

Let's see what the final code for this example will look like:

```
package coreJavaTraining;

public class Firstclass {

    public void getData()
    {
        System.out.println(" I am in method")
    }
    public static void main(String[] args)
    {
        Firstclass fn=new Firstclass();
        fn.getData();
        System.out.println("hi");
        System.out.println("hello world");
    }
}
```

So if we run the class given in the example, our result will be as follows:

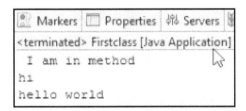

Output displaying I am in method as per the code

`I am in method` is what we see in the output; this is because control starts from the memory-allocation line, creates an object, and using the object we call the method of that class. Control goes back to the `getData()` block and completes the lines of code that are present in that particular block; it executes the print statement, and we see that it gets printed. This is why objects are powerful in calling a method.

The same technique can be used for calling integers. Let's say we declare a variable in the a class and assign a value to it. We can print the variable value by adding the following line in the `main` method:

```
System.out.println(fn.a);
```

This is one way of using classes, objects, and methods in Java; basically we are encapsulating.

Accessing a method in a different class

Let's say we face a situation where we are working with one class and we need to access an object in another class; this can be done in Java. Let's use an example to help explain this. Let's use two classes, `Firstclass()` (from the *Accessing an object in Java* section), and we'll create a new class, called `secondclass()`. On creating a new class, the default code is created by the editor and we're able to add code in it. We add a random method, `public void setData()`, within which we print the `I am in second class method` statement.

Now, we want the `setData()` method in the `Firstclass()` class. Basically we want to execute the `setData()` method in `Firstclass()`. And methods can be called only with the objects of that particular class. To do so, we create an object in the method that calls the method in the other class. We use similar code to what we used in the previous example to allocate memory for an object. The following code is added in the `main` method of `Firstclass()`:

```
secondclass sn= new secondclass();
sn.setData();
```

While typing the code in the `main` class, when we type `sn.` to call the method, we will again get all the choices of methods that there are in Java. Since we want to call `setData()`, we select it from the multiple options that are shared with us. This will successfully bring `setData()` into in the `main` method of `Firstclass()` by creating an object for the class.

If we run the code, we will get the following output:

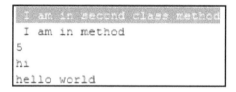

I am in second class method
I am in method
5
hi
hello world

Output displaying I am in second class method as per the code

Summary

We started off by discussing the difference between strings and variables, and how they appear in a code. We then saw what methods are and how can they be used to write our code. After that, we discussed the importance of classes and objects, and how they are used to call methods that execute a class. We learned how to allocate memory to an object and call the method of that object while executing the code.Finally, we learned how to access a method that is present in another class using objects.

In the next chapter we will learn more about strings and have a look at the `String` class.

3
Handling Strings and Their Functions in Java

In this chapter, we'll talk about strings and have a look at the `String` class. We will also learn how to define a string and look at the different ways in which we can define a string. We will then discuss the different methods in the `String` class. Lastly, we will write some simple code to reverse the contents of a string, and we will also check whether or not that reversed string is a palindrome.

We will cover the following topics in this chapter:

- Introducing strings
- The String class and its methods
- Reversing a string's logic

Introducing strings

A string is one of the most important concepts in Java programming. `String` is one of the prebuilt classes in Java. So if you want to manipulate strings, then you could simply create an object of this `String` class, and using that object, you can manipulate the string however you want. You can then break the string into two parts, based on the `substring` concept. We can also concatenate two strings. All of this can be done with the help of this `String` class.

Let's try manipulating a string ourselves. Create a new Java class and name it `stringclassdemo`.

One of the most common questions asked in almost all Java related interviews is how a programmer can define strings. The answer is that you can use either of the two following ways:

- By defining the `String` literal
- By creating an object of `String`

Now let's look at each method, one by one, in order to understand the different ways of declaring a string.

Defining the String literal

Defining the `String` literal can be done simply, as follows:

```
String a= "hello";
```

We created a string, which is `hello`, and stored it in the variable called `a`. This is how we define a `String`, which is the same as defining the `String` literal.

Let's say that you have defined one more string, as follows:

```
String a= "hello";
String b= "hello";
```

Unfortunately, even the `b` variable has a `hello` string, and the `a` variable also has the same string defined. When the Java program compiles this, it creates one `String` object called `a`, and assigns `hello`.

Now, before creating an object for this `hello` string, the `b` variable first checks whether there is any `hello` string instance already defined in the `String` pool. If it is already defined, it simply refers `a` to the `b` object rather than creating one more object separately.

Creating an object of the String class

We create an object of the `String` class as shown in the following line of code:

```
String ab=new String();
```

Now, to create a `hello` string, you could simply pass an argument into the `String` class, as follows:

```
String ab=new String("hello");
```

The `ab` object can now perform all the string manipulations on this `hello` string.

Let's create another string, called `b`, which also equals to `hello`, as follows:

```
String a=new String("hello");
String b=new String("hello");
```

Here, though, there is already one `hello` string created with the `a` object, and when the Java compiler comes to the `b` object, it will still create one more duplicate `hello` string and assign it to `b`, because here we are explicitly forcing it to create an object for this class. Although there is a duplicate already present, it will still create an object for this string; however, in defining a `String` literal, if the object is already present in the `String` pool, it will not create it—instead, it directly refers it to the already created object.

So that's the basic difference between creating a string with the `String` literal object and separately creating an object with the `String` class. Ultimately, both support `String` methods, but there is some difference between the two methods when it comes to defining a string.

What is the difference between these two methods that we just learned? Both strings have access to the `hello` string, but you can see that there is some difference between them. If you declare the string in the literal fashion at the backend, then Java assigns `hello` to the `a` variable. So this is a more direct way of creating a string, rather than using the object creation method.

In most of our regular Java working experience, we would prefer to use the `String` literal. We just state that `a` equals `hello`, and that's it. It's just like how you define integers. But `String` is a class, and at the backend, it creates a separate object for this `hello` string, whereas an integer is just a reference data type, so nothing will happen at its backend.

Let's see what manipulations we can apply to this `hello` string with the object we created.

The String class and its methods

We have the `a` variable, and this variable also acts an object. When we type `a.` in the editor, it'll show all the methods that are present in that `String` class, as shown in the following screenshot:

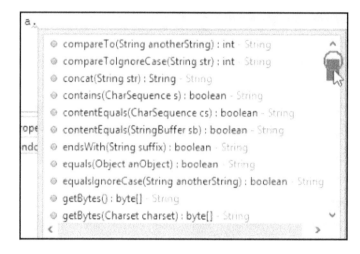

It reads the first character in the strings as index zero, the second character as index one, and so on. When working on a program, if you want the character present on index two, you can get it simply by using the following statement:

```
Systme.out.println(a.charAt(2));
```

You print it in the output so that you will see that character. You might be wondering why would we need a single character from a string, but the `charAt` method is often used. In the next section, we will look at a program that can completely reverse the string.

For now, we will just go through an overview of the methods. We saw how to get a character that is present at a particular index position. Now let's try reversing this. Say that we have the character present and we need to find the index value at which the character is present in the string. We do this by using the `indexOf` method, shown as follows:

```
Systme.out.println(a.indexOf"e"));
```

Run this program. You can see that the character 1 is at 2, H is at 0, e is at index 1, and l is at index 2. This is how you can extract characters and indexes with the help of the String methods.

But what if I want to pull the string only from the first character to the third character? Let's take a look at the following example:

```
String a= "javatraining";
a.substring(3, 6);
```

We type a., and you can see that there is a substring. If you want to pull a string that starts at index 3 and ends at index 6, this means that j will be at 0, a will be at 1, and so on. It starts from 2, and moves on to 3, 4, and 5, and it will print something like vatra.

If you want to pull out substring from the entire string, then give the first letter index and the last letter index so that our entire string will be printed between that first and last letter. Bear in mind that there is another substring method, and with this method, if you don't pass the last index, passing only the first index, then it prints from index 5 to the last index, as follows:

```
a.substring(5);
```

Let's print the output and see how the substring is extracted. The results of this are shown in the following screenshot:

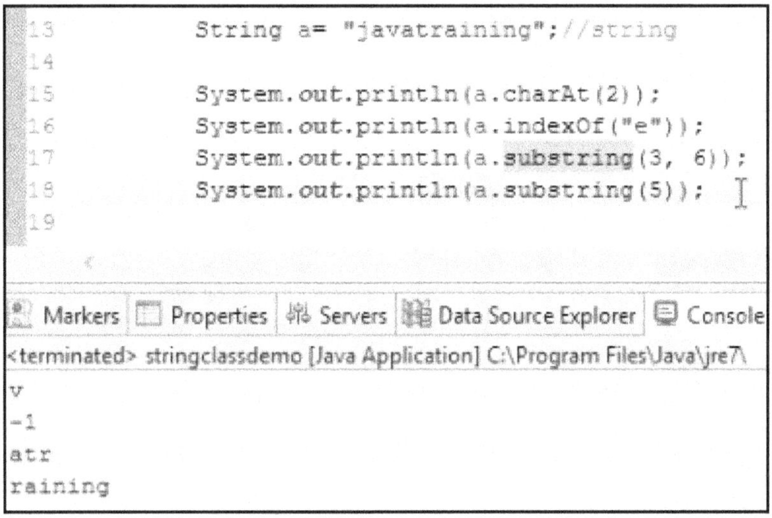

Here, the index of e is -1, because there is no alphabetical character called e in this string. Whenever there is nothing, then it prints a -1.

That sums up substring. If I want to concat this string with one more string called rahul teaches, then I do the following:

```
String a= "javatraining";
System.out.priontln(a.concat("rahul teaches"));
```

The javatraining string that is present in the a variable will be concatenated with rahul teaches, and it prints the output as javatrainingrahul teaches. We can also use a.length(), which will give the maximum length of this string starting from zero. There is one more type called trim. Let's say that there are some white spaces in your string, as follows:

```
String a= " javatraining";
System.out.println(a.trim());
```

Here, the first character of the string is a blank space, and is then followed by the rest of the characters. If you want to remove that blank space, you can do so by simply using a.trim. This blank space is removed when you print the output.

If you want to print all the letters in uppercase, we can use a.toUpperCase. We can do the same for lowercase by using a.toLowerCase.

There is one more interesting method to look at, which is split. Basically, we can split the entire string based on our delimiter. For this, we use a.split(). In this case, we want to split it based on a slash in the code, as follows:

```
String a= "java/training";
System.out.println(a.split(/));
```

This means that the whole string before the / character should be separated as one string and the remaining part should be separated as another string. This method can not only be used to split across a slash, but can also split across whatever we want it to, as shown in the following code:

```
String a= "javatraining";
System.out.println(a.split(t));
```

If we want to split our string from t, then that means that java will be one string and raining will be another string. As we will have two strings, our output will store these two strings in an array, and this array return type will be, of course, a String, because it's written in a String, as shown in the following code:

```
String arr[]=a.split("t");
System.out.println(arr[0]);
System.out.println(arr[1]);
```

If you want to print the first part of the string, then this will be stored in the 0 index of the array system, and if you want to print the second part of the string, then it will present it in the 1 index of the array.

One final method that we will discuss here is the replace method, shown in the following code:

```
String a= "javatraining";
System.out.println(a.replace("t", "s"));
```

Here, we want to replace the t from the string with a random s. For this, we use a.replace("t", "s"), and that's it. On printing this, wherever a t is present in the string, it will be changed to an s, and it will be printed in your output.

That's pretty much it for String methods. You could still play around with them by using a. and go through different methods step by step, but these are the core methods that we use in our Java programming.

Let's try to tackle one example based on the methods that we have learned in this section.

Reversing a string's logic

In this section, let's see how we can print a string in reverse. This is one of the questions that was asked in the Yahoo interview. Let's create a reversedemo class for our example.

We have a string called Rahul, and we want the output to be luhaR. There is one more concept that we need to be aware of: a palindrome. If you type in a string, such as madam, and we reverse the string, it would just give madam as the output. Such types of strings are called **palindromes**. One such instance of a palindrome is shown in the following code:

```
package demopack;

public class reversedemo {
    public static void main(String[] args) {
```

```java
String s = "madam";
String t= "";
for(int i=s.length()-1; i>=0; i--)
{
    t= t+ s.charAt(i);
}
System.out.println(t);
    }
}
```

We would start by creating a string, called s, and an empty string, called t. We create this empty string to concatenate each element after the for loop to get the output in the console in the form of a string; otherwise, we may get it something like the following:

m
a
d
a
m

Using the concatenation logic, we can display the output as follows:

madam

This was a simple logic that is used to reverse our string and display it in the form of a string using the empty string logic. We used the charAt method and implemented our reverse string. Once we have our reverse string, we can easily compare it with the original string—in our case, this involves comparing the t string with the s string, and if they both match, then we can print that the given string is a palindrome.

Forget about palindromes. This is the concept of string reversal.

Summary

In this chapter, we were introduced to strings, which are one of the more important classes in Java. We looked at the different ways to define a string. We then looked at the different methods that come under the String class. We looked at some of the most commonly used methods in the String class, and in the final section, we looked at an example of reversing a string to better understand the String class.

In the next chapter we will understand the important loops and conditions through examples.

4
Building Blocks for Java Programs – Loops and Conditions

Loops and conditions are the building blocks of Java programs. This chapter will help us understand the important loops and conditions through examples. Learning these loops and conditions in Java will make writing code easier.

In this chapter, we will cover the following topics:

- The for loop
- The if...else condition
- The while loop
- Nested loops

The for loop

Let's see how the for loop works. The for loop is one of the most commonly used loops in Java programs, and it it is very important to understand how it works internally. So, let's say we want to print the numbers from 1 to 100 using the forloop. For the syntax to execute the numbers from 1 to 100 in a sequence and to write that in a for loop, we will simply write:

```
// 1 to 100

/*  for(initialization;condition;increment)
    {
    } */
    for (int i=0;i<100;i++)
```

```
        {
              system.out.println(i);
        }
}
```

Since we want to print 0, 1, 2, 3, we use `i++`. This means for every loop, it increments only by `1`. And while looping, each time, it also checks whether the preceding condition is satisfied. So, if `1` is less than `100`, it goes inside; if `2` is less than `100`, it goes inside. Until this condition is satisfied, it will keep on looping. When the value of `i` reaches `100`, `100` is less than `100`, which is false. At that time, it terminates the loop and comes out of it. We will use a basic example here:

```
for (int i=0;i<5;i++)
    {
          system.out.println(i);
    }
```

To run test cases in debug mode in the IDE, double-click at the location shown in the following screenshot:

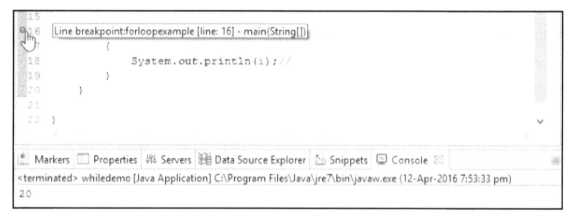

Line from which the debugging begins

When you see the blue icon, run that in the debug mode by clicking the insects-like symbol. It will ask you to launch in debug mode. Just click on Save to do so:

Debug icon at the top of the editor

You will see all the variable values here. Step by step, we'll go inside the loop, and will execute the next step of the program:

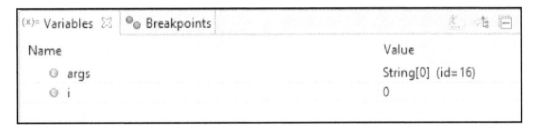

Variable value while debugging

Finally, when it reaches the value 4, and is incremented by 1 again, it is 5. Note that it comes out of the loop without going inside that after the value becomes 5. So, that means the condition is no longer satisfied and the loop will run five times. The output is shown in the following screenshot:

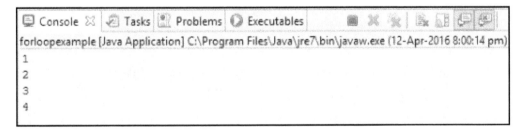

Final output as per the code

So, that's how the for loop works.

Now, if we set the condition to the following, it will not go inside the `for` loop, even for the first time since, the condition is false.:

```
for (int i=5;i<3;i++)
```

On running the preceding condition in in the debug mode, the complete loop is skipped,and nothing is seen in the output.

Let's see another example:

```
for (int i=0;i<10;i+2 )
```

The output will be:

```
0
2
4
6
8
```

This is how the `for` loop works internally.

In the next section, we will learn about the `if...else` and `do...while` loops.

if...else condition

Before we learn the `while` and `do...while` loops, we will discuss the `if` condition in this section. In a Java program, when the `if` conditional statement is used, the statement in the `if` block is executed only if the condition is satisfied. Otherwise the statement from `else` block is run. Also this execution is just takes place once. In a `for` loop, a variable is initiated and the loop runs till the condition is satisfied.

However, in the `if` case, it will not keep on looping. It will just go inside the loop once the `if` condition is satisfied; otherwise, it will go into the `else` block. So, control will execute the statements present in this `else` block, as shown in the following screenshot:

```
15          if(true)
16          {
17
18          }
19          else
20          {
21
22          }
23
24          for(int i=0;i<10;i=i+2)
25          {
26              System.out.println(i);//
27          }
28      }
29
```

Markers   Properties   Servers   Data Source Explorer   Snippets   Console

<terminated> forloopexample [Java Application] C:\Program Files\Java\jre7\bin\javaw.exe (12-Apr-2016 8:03:53 pm)

Output of the if...else condition as per the code

But all this happens only once, unlike the `for` loop, where a condition is satisfied until it goes back and executes.

Let's take a look at the following example:

```
if(5>2)
{
    System.out.println("success");
}
else
{
    System.out.println("fail");
}
```

The following screenshot displays those errors:

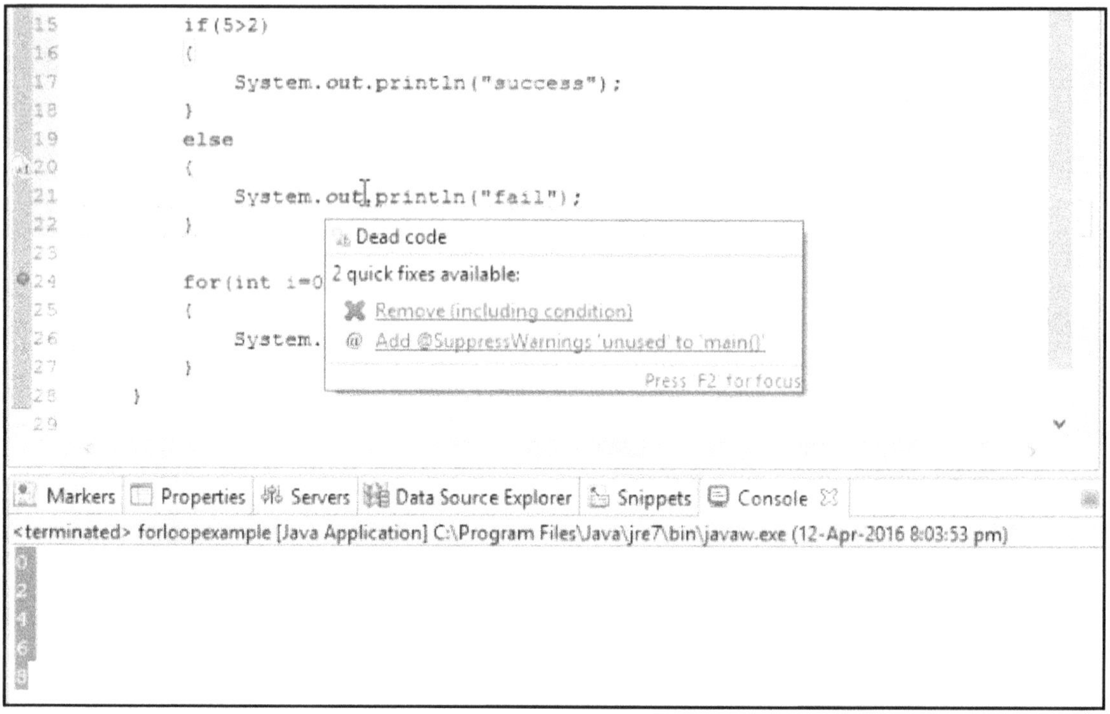

```
15          if(5>2)
16          {
17              System.out.println("success");
18          }
19          else
20          {
21              System.out.println("fail");
22          }
23
24          for(int i=0
25          {
26              System.
27          }
28      }
29
```

Dead code
2 quick fixes available:
✖ Remove (including condition)
@ Add @SuppressWarnings 'unused' to 'main()'
Press F2 for focus

🔲 Markers 🔲 Properties 🔲 Servers 🔲 Data Source Explorer 🔲 Snippets 🔲 Console ✕
<terminated> forloopexample [Java Application] C:\Program Files\Java\jre7\bin\javaw.exe (12-Apr-2016 8:03:53 pm)
0
2
4
6
8

Quick fixes drop down with suggestions to correct the code error

The first error is to remove the including condition, which can be ignored. On running the preceding program, you will see the output as `success` because the condition 5 greater than 2 that went inside is true:

```
15          if(5>2)
16          {
17              System.out.println("success");
18          }
19          else
20          {
21              System.out.println("fail");
22          }
23
24          for(int i=0;i<10;i=i+2)
25          {
26              System.out.println(i);//
27          }
28      }
29
```

| Markers | Properties | Servers | Data Source Explorer | Snippets | Console |

```
<terminated> forloopexample [Java Application] C:\Program Files\Java\jre7\bin\javaw.exe (12-Apr-2016 8:06:49 pm)
success
0
2
4
6
8
```

Output displays success as per the code

If we change the condition and make 5 less than 2, making the condition false, it will skip to the `else` block and execute the statement present in `else`.

```
15          if(5<2)
16          {
17              System.out.println("success");
18          }
19          else
20          {
21              System.out.println("fail");
22          }
23
24          for(int i=0;i<10;i=i+2)
25          {
26              System.out.println(i);//
27          }
28      }
29
```

code to receive fail as the output

This time the output should be `fail`, as shown in the following screenshot:

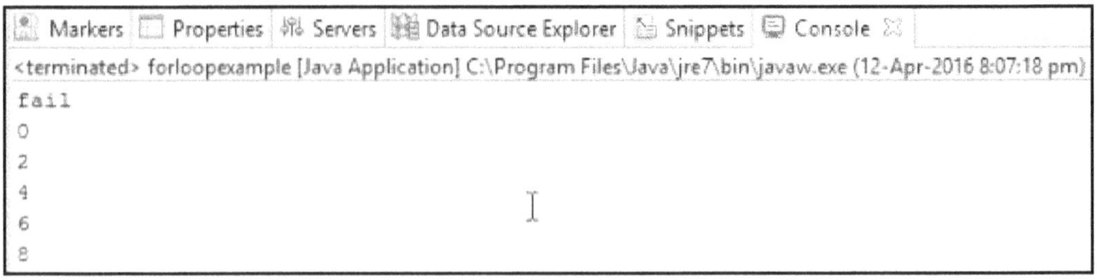

Output displays success as per the code

This is how the `if` condition works.

Note that if there is only a single line in your block, then you can get rid of these braces, because it eventually assumes that the next line will be executed if the condition is true. This means if you just have a single line in your block, then you can get rid of the braces. But if you want to have more than one statement, if your condition is true, then make sure you write that in braces to avoid conflict. If you do not specify the braces, it will still print as `success`, as shown in the following screenshot:

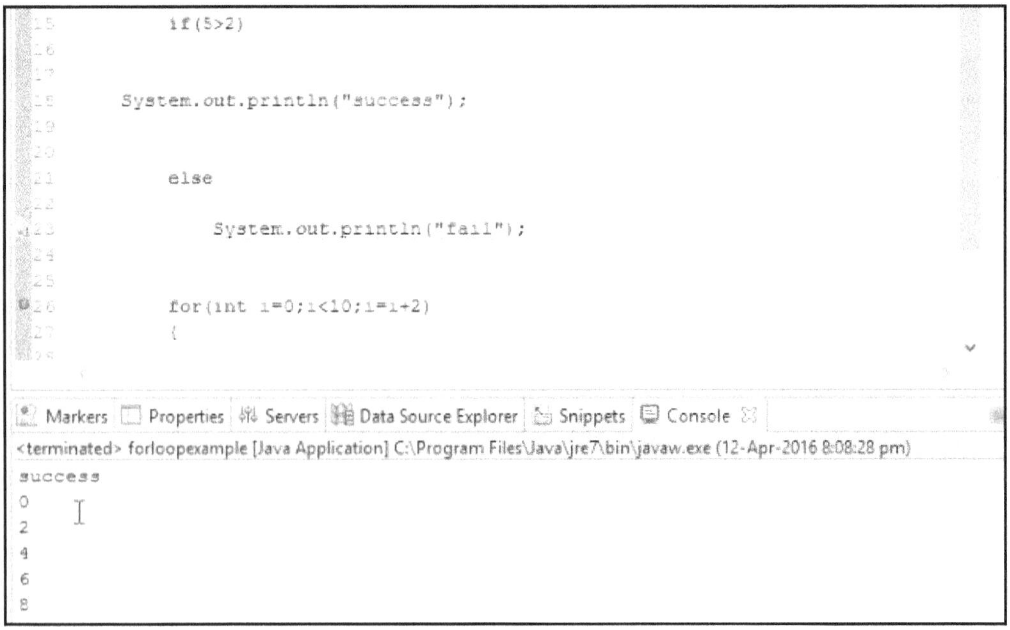

Output displays success after modifying the code

Here, 5 is greater than 2. On running this, the program will run without braces.

Now, on adding one more statement, say "second step", it throws an error, as shown in the following screenshot:

```
15          if(5>2)
16
17
18      System.out.println("success");
19          System.out.println("second step");
20
21          else
22             ⊗ Syntax error on token "else", delete this token
23                                      Press F2 for focus
24
25
26          for(int i=0;i<10;i=i+2)
27          {
28             System.out.println(i);//
29          }
30      }
31
32  }
```

Markers | Properties | Servers | Data Source Explorer | Snippets | Console ⊠

<terminated> forloopexample [Java Application] C:\Program Files\Java\jre7\bin\javaw.exe (12-Apr-2016 8:08:28 pm)

```
success
0
2
4
6
8
```

Error is flagged with a cross mark besides the line number, showing syntax error

Notice the syntax error on the token in the preceding screenshot. Either you should keep a brace or you should avoid this step. To get rid of that, we will just keep the entire block in the brace. In this way, the error goes away.

Bringing the if...else condition in the for loop

Now, let us bring the if...else condition into the for loop. Let's add the following to our code:

```
for (int i=0;i<10;i=i+2)
{
```

```
        if(i==8)
        system.out.println("print 8 is displayed");
        else
            system.out.println("I did not find");
    }
```

Since there is only one statement here, we won't be writing it in the braces. Now, let's analyze this. The values will begin to enter the `for` loop from zero until the value is less than `10`.

On entering the `for` loop, it will check if the first value, `0`, is equal to `8`. Since it is not equal, it will display `"I didnot find"`. Now, for the second time, `2` will be added to `0` (as per our set condition). Notice that this new value is still not equal to `8`; hence the output will remain same for values `0`, `2`, `4`, and `6`. Next, when `8` goes inside the `for` loop, the condition is satisfied and the `" 8 is displayed"` statement is displayed as the output:

"8 is displayed" and "I didnot find" is displayed as the output

Now, if we say `i=9`, it will never be printed because the condition we set is `i+2`, which will be an incremental even number. This means that the condition is not satisfied and the very next step after the `if` condition is not executed. Thus, we can say that, if a condition is true, only then will it be executed; if not, the conditions or the statements present in the `else` block will be executed. And when you run this, you always get the output as `"I did not find"`.

However, if we write the following syntax, we will get the output as `"9 is displayed"`:

```
for(int i=0;i<10;i=i+3)
```

This is how the `if...else` condition works using the `for` loop. In the next section, we will learn about `for` loops in detail.

The while loop

In this section, we will learn the `while` loop in detail. First, create a new class. Now let us see how we can utilize this `while` loop when programming our code. Let's say we want to print the numbers from 1 to 10, sequentially. How do we print this using the `while` loop? The basic syntax of the `while` loop is:

```
// While loop

while(boolean)
{

}
```

And here, if the Boolean expression returns `true`, only then will the control go inside this loop, whereas if the expression returns `false`, then the control will not go inside the loop. That's the basic simple concept you have with the `while` loop. Now let's say we want to bring in the numbers from 1 to 10. For this, we will write the following code:

```
//While loop

//1 to 10

int i=0;
while(i<10)
{
        System.out.println(i);
}
```

As you can see, in the preceding code example, we can see that that the given condition is true. So, it goes inside the loop and prints the value of `i`. This loop keeps on executing until the expression evaluates to false. As per our example, the condition will always be true; thus, it will go to the infinite loop and print zero.

This is how the `while` loop works. Unless the condition becomes false in this argument, this loop will never stop executing. Now, what if we increment after printing the variable? Let's see what happens when we do that:

```
//While loop

//1 to 10

int i=0;
while(i<10)
{
        System.out.println(i);
        i++;
}
```

The output will be as that shown in the following screenshot:

```
whiledemo.java ⌧
1  package coreJava;
2
3  public class whiledemo {
4
5      public static void main(String[] args) {
6          // TODO Auto-generated method stub
7
8
9          //While loop
10
11         //1 to 10
12         int i=0;
13
14         while(i<10)
15         {
16             System.out.println(i);
17             i++;//i=2
18         }
19     }
20
21 }
22
```

```
Markers    Properties   Servers   Data Source Explorer   Snippets   Console ⌧
<terminated> whiledemo [Java Application] C:\Program Files\Java\jre7\bin\javaw.exe (12-Apr-2016 7:45:24 pm)
5
6
7
8
9
```

Output of the while condition as per the code

If we use the following condition:

```
while(i<=10)
```

The new output will be:

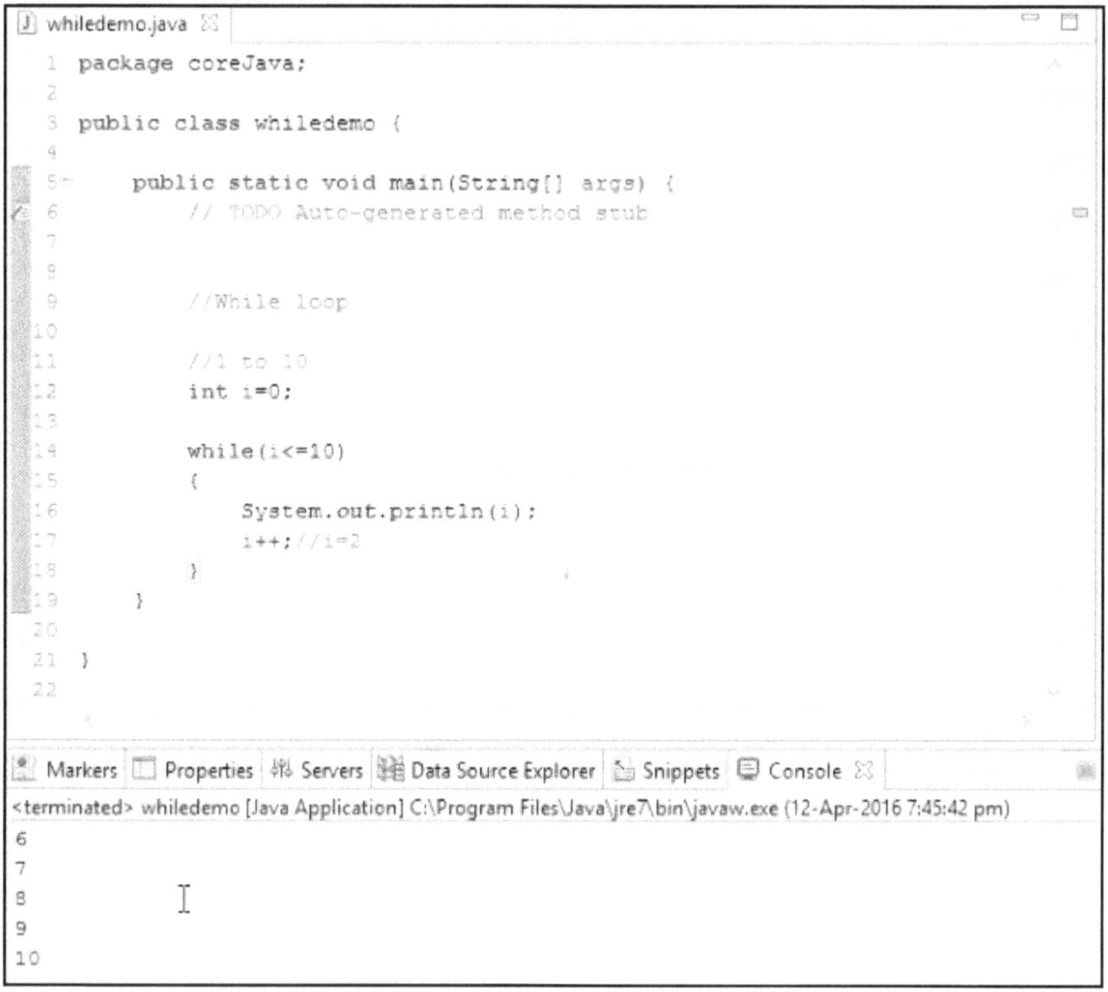

```java
package coreJava;

public class whiledemo {

    public static void main(String[] args) {
        // TODO Auto-generated method stub


        //While loop

        //1 to 10
        int i=0;

        while(i<=10)
        {
            System.out.println(i);
            i++;//i=2
        }
    }

}
```

Markers Properties Servers Data Source Explorer Snippets Console

```
<terminated> whiledemo [Java Application] C:\Program Files\Java\jre7\bin\javaw.exe (12-Apr-2016 7:45:42 pm)
6
7
8
9
10
```

Output of the while condition after modifying the code

Similarly, you you can reverse the condition, as follows:

```java
//While loop

//1 to 10

int i=10;
while(i>0)
```

```
    {
        System.out.println(i);
        i++;//i=2
    }
```

The output will go to infinite, since the numbers keep on increasing because 10 is greater than 0.

If we use the decrement condition, it will keep on decreasing until the condition becomes false. After that, it will exit the loop, as shown in the following code example:

```
//While loop

//1 to 10

int i=10;
while(i>0)
{
        System.out.println(i);
        i--;//i=2
}
```

The output for the preceding code example will be:

```
5
4
3
2
1
```

So, this is how we can use the `while` loop syntax in our Java program. In the next section, we will see how to work on the `do...while` loop.

The do...while loop

The syntax of the `do...while` loop is:

```
do
{
}while();
```

Let's consider the following example, where we want to print the numbers from 20 to 30:

```
    int j=20;
do
{
```

```
    j++;
}while(j<30); // 1 loop of execution is guaranteed
```

The preceding code will print 20, 21, 22 until 29 as the output. Thus, first it executes and then it compares.

The basic difference between the `while` and `do...while` loop is that the `while` loop will not execute without evaluating the Boolean expression, and the `do...while` loop first executes for one loop and then evaluates to run for more loops.

Let's consider the following example, where the value of the variable is greater than 30:

```
int j=20;
do
{
    j++;
}while(j>30); // 1 loop of execution is guaranteed
```

Here, the output will be 20, while the script after that will be terminated because, as mentioned earlier in this section, in the `do...while` loop, execution of one loop is guaranteed. If you run same logic in this `while` loop, even for the first time, it will not run.

So, in the next section, we will try to do one exercise based on the `for` loop, the `while` loop, the `do...while` loop, and the `if` condition. These programs will be good hands-on learning for understanding the loops.

In the next section, we will learn how the nested loops work.

Nested loops

This is one of the most important concepts. All the programming logic comes from the nested loops. If you can grasp the concept behind it, it will be easy for you to solve the programming examples in Java. So, first of all, I will write one syntax:

```
for(int i=1;i<=4;i++)  // this block will loop for 4 times
{
}
```

The preceding syntax means that the loop will run four times. What if we write one more `for` loop inside the preceding block? The concept of implementing a loop within a loop is called **nested loops**:

```
        for(int i=1;i<=4;i++)
        // (outer for loop) it will loop for 4 times
```

```
{
    System.out.println("outer loop started");
    for(int j=1;j<=4;j++) //(inner for loop)
    {
        System.out.println("inner loop");
    }
    System.out.println("outer loop finished");
}
```

Thus, one looping system is completed when we finish the preceding iteration once. To finish one outer loop, we have to complete all four inner loops. This means that we will have to run this inner loop 16 times (four times four) to just finish this outer loop four times.

The output is shown in the following screenshot:

Output of the nested loops as per the code

Further ahead, the concept of `for` loops will be used more often. To understand the concept of `for` loops, let's try to solve a few examples.

Example 1

Write the code for the following output:

```
1 2 3 4
5 6 7
8 9
10
```

As we can observe in the output, for every line, one number is decrementing. We will look at the concept of the outer loop and inner loop here. The code will be as follows:

```
int k=1;
for(int i=0;i<4;i++)
// (outer for loop) it will loop for 4 times
    {
        //System.out.println("outer loop started");
        for(int j=1;j<=4;j++) //(inner for loop)
        {
            System.out.print("k");
            System.out.print("\t");
        }
        System.out.println(" ");
    }
```

Example 2

Write the code for the following output:

```
1
2 3
4 5 6
7 8 9 10
```

As you can see, the output used in this example is the reverse of the output from first example:

```
int k=1;
for(int i=1;i<5;i++)
// (outer for loop) it will loop for 4 times
    {
        //System.out.println("outer loop started");
        for(int j=1;j<=i;j++) //(inner for loop)
        {
            System.out.print("k");
            System.out.print("\t");
            k++;
        }
        System.out.println(" ");
    }
```

Example 3

In a similar fashion, there is one more program, called sorting numbers

Write the code for the following output:

```
1
1 2
1 2 3
1 2 3 4
```

The code for the preceding output will be:

```
for(int i=1;i<5;i++)
// (outer for loop) it will loop for 4 times
    {
        for(int j=1;j<=i;j++) //(inner for loop)
        {
            System.out.print("j");
            System.out.print("\t");
        }
        System.out.println(" ");
    }
```

Summary

With the use of easy examples, we learned how to use the `if...else` condition in Java. We also saw how to use the `for` loop and the `while` loops to get the desired outputs. Moving further ahead, we learned how to use the nested `for` loops to get the outputs in certain patterns.

In the next chapter, we will go through some important concepts, such as interfaces, how they work, and their usage in Java. We will also discuss inheritance using a practical example.

5
Everything You Need to Know About Interfaces and Inheritance

In this chapter, we will go through some important concepts, such as interfaces, how they work, and their usage in Java. We will discuss inheritance using a practical example. This chapter will also look at the concepts of function overloading and function overriding and the differences between them.

We will cover the following topics in this chapter:

- Interfaces
- Introduction to inheritance
- Function overloading
- Function overriding

Interfaces

The interface is one of the core concepts used in Java OOPS, so it's necessary for us to familiarize ourselves with interfaces and their use.

Interfaces are similar to classes. The only difference between an interface and a class is that an interface will have methods but not a body. Confused? In a class, we generally define a method and then start writing code into it. For example, in a class, if we want to write any code, we just start off by declaring the class using `public void` and proceed with the rest of the code in that class, as follows:

```
public void getData()
{
}
```

In interfaces, we can only define the signature of the method; we cannot write any code inside the method. But why? What is the use of writing a method signature inside an interface? What is the use of this object-oriented concept in Java? You might have these questions in your mind, so let's try to understand the concept of the interface with a real-life scenario.

Using interfaces with a traffic light system

Consider the typical traffic light system, which is used everywhere around the world to maintain traffic regulations. Every country has its own traffic rules, such as driving on the left or right side of the road. Even though traffic rules differ from country to country, there are certain rules that apply globally and need to be followed by every country. One such rule is the use of traffic lights to govern the traffic flow, where a red light is an indication to stop, an amber/yellow light to ready your engine, and a green light to move your vehicle. Let's say that these global rules are imposed by a central traffic authority, and we want to implement, for example, the Australian traffic system. This system will have its own rules, but we need to make sure that it follows the global rules imposed by the central traffic authority.

Using this example, we'll try to understand the concept of interfaces. Here, the central traffic authority acts as an interface and the Australian traffic rules act as a class that implements the interface; that is, the Australian traffic system will have to follow the rules/methods mentioned in the central traffic authority interface. The methods defined in any interface are just signatures, so the classes will define and implement the methods present in an interface. Let's look at this example in our Java code.

We define an interface in the same way that we define a class. In this traffic light example, let's name the class as `CentralTraffic`. We now have a ready interface, as follows:

```
package demopack;

public interface CentralTraffic {
```

```
    public void greenGo();
    public void redStop();
    public void FlashYellow();


}
```

We can see in the syntax that instead of `class` we have written `interface`. We define a method in the interface using the same method that we use to define a method in a class, but remember that we cannot have a method body defining the method as this is an interface, and doing so will throw an error. Create another class to implement this interface and name it `AustralianTraffic`. Once we have a Java class, we need to implement the `CentralTraffic` interface to it, and we do that using the `implements` keyword, as follows:

```
public class AustralianTraffic implements CentralTraffic {
```

After using the preceding sentence, our IDE will show an error, and when you hover over the error, you'll see some suggestions related to the error. One suggestion would be to import `CentralTraffic`, and another would be to add unimplemented methods. Click on these suggestions to resolve the error and you should end up with the following code:

```
package coreJava;
import demopack.CentralTraffic;
public class AustralianTraffic implements CentralTraffic {

    public static void main(String[] args) {
    }
    @Override
    public void greenGo() {
        // TODO Auto-generated method stub
        System.out.println(" greengo implementation")
    }
    @Override
    public void redStop() {
        // TODO Auto-generated method stub
        System.out.println(" redstop implementation")
    }
    @Override
    public void FlashingYellow() {
        // TODO Auto-generated method stub
        System.out.println(" flash yellow implementation")
    }

}
```

All the methods defined in the `CentralTraffic` interface can be seen in the `AustralianTraffic` class, and here we can also implement these methods as we wish. Now, if we remove the `greenGo` method from our Java class, it'll give us an error. As it is a method defined in an interface, it is mandatory for us to implement all the methods defined in the interface.

The interface methods are defined outside `public static void main`, and to execute these methods, we should create a class object for them in the `main` method, as follows:

```
CentralTraffic a= new AustralianTraffic();
```

This line of code says that we have created an object for the `AustralianTraffic` class to implement the methods present in the `CentralTraffic` interface. The main class should look as follows:

```
public class AustralianTraffic implements CentralTraffic {

    public static void main(String[] args) {
    CentralTraffic a= new AustralianTraffic();
    a.redStop();
    a.FlashYellow();
    a.greenGo();
    }
```

Now, after implementing the methods from the interface, we can define our own country-specific methods (rules) in our Java class, as follows:

```
public void walkonsymbol()
{
    System.out.println("walking");
}
```

In our `main` method, if we try calling our country-specific method using `a.`, like we did for the other methods in the `main` class, then we will find that we won't be able to do so because the `walkonsymbol` method is specific to a particular country (that is, the `AustralianTraffic` class) and it's not implemented in `CentralTraffic`. For the `walkonsymbol` method, we need to create another object in the `main` class specific to the `AustralianTraffic` class, as follows:

```
AustralianTraffic at=new AustralianTraffic();
at.walkonsymbol();
```

Another piece of information related to the interface is that a class can implement more than one interface. Let's say that we create another interface, such as `ContinentalTraffic`, and define another rule related to traffic lights, such as a train symbol to indicate that a train is passing by. We can implement this interface in our `AustralianTraffic` class simply by adding a comma, as follows:

```
public class AustralianTraffic implements CentralTraffic,
ContinentalTraffic {
```

For this interface, we need to follow the same steps as we did for the `CentralTraffic` interface, such as importing `ContinentalTraffic` to `AustralianTraffic`, adding unimplemented methods, creating an object specific to `ContinentalTraffic` in the main class, and so on.

Now you have a fair idea of the differences between an interface and a class. We learned how to define the interfaces, how to implement them within another class, and how to call them using objects.

Inheritance

Inheritance is another important OOP concept in Java. Let's take an example of a vehicle to understand the concept of inheritance, just like we did in using the example of a traffic light system to understand interfaces. The basic properties of a vehicle are its color, gears, mirrors, brakes, and so on. Let's say that we are making a new vehicle with certain advancements to some of these properties, such as an engine with a higher CC, and maybe a different design than the old one. Now, to create a new vehicle with these new features, we still need the basic features of the old vehicle, such as mirrors and brakes, which are present in vehicles by default.

Let's take the preceding example and use Java to reflect these relationships in order to understand the concept of inheritance. In our example, if we have a class for a vehicle and enter the basic features of the vehicle as methods that are present in that class, then when we create a class for a new vehicle, it can inherit the features of the class that is created for the vehicle, and we don't have to write the code for these features as they are available to us via inheritance.

Let's get started with the code. Create a `parentClassdemo` class, which will be our parent class. In this class, we will define our methods, as follows:

```
package coreJava;
public class parentClassdemo {
    String color = "red";
```

```
        public void Gear()
        {
            System.out.println("gear code is implemented");
        }
        public void Brakes()
        {
            System.out.println("brakes code is implemented");
        }
        public void audiosystem()
        {
            System.out.println("audiosystem code is implemented");
        }
    }
```

We will now inherit these methods in our child class. Create a `childClassDemo` in Java. We inherit the parent class using the `extends` keyword, as follows:

```
package coreJava;
public class childClassDemo extends parentClassdemo {

    public void engine()
    {
        System.out.println("new engine");
    }
    public void color
    {
        System.out.println(color);
    }

    public static void main(String[] args) {
        childClassDemo cd=new childClassDemo();
        cd.color();
    }
}
```

Here, we inherited the `parentClassdemo` class in the `childClassDemo` class using the `extends` keyword. In this `childClassDemo` class, we defined our own `engine` method and used the `color` method, which we inherited from the `parentClassdemo` class. We then created a `cd` object and used it to call the methods from the inherited class.

More on inheritance

Let's discuss some notorious tricky questions and misconceptions regarding inheritance in Java.

Let's get started with some of the more well-known questions asked concerning inheritance. Take a look at the following block of code:

```
class X
{
    //Class X members
}

class Y
{
    //Class Y members
}

class Z extends X, Y
{
    //Class Z members
}
```

In the preceding code snippet, we have the X and Y class and some data fields or methods inside it. The Z class inherits the X and Y classes. Is this allowed? The answer is no. Java does not allows multiple inheritances, whereas it is allowed in C++. So here, we can conclude that the preceding code snippet is not right and will throw an error.

This is also one of the differences between inheritance and interfaces, as an interface allows us to use multiple interfaces at a time.

Take a look at the following example:

```
class A
{
    int i = 10;
}

class B extends A
{
    int i = 20;
}

public class MainClass
{
    public static void main(String[] args)
    {
        A a = new B();
        System.out.println(a.i);
    }
}
```

Here, we have an A class and it has an i variable. There is also a B class that extends the A class, and we also have its local i variable set as 20. Now, in MainClass, we create an object for the B class. What does this step actually mean? Here, we are creating an object and saying that this object of this B class should refer to the properties of the A class. Though we have permission to access this B class through this a object, we can only access the properties or methods of the A class, because the B class has permission to access the A class here, as we are extending it.

The question here is what will a.i print—20 or 10? The answer is, it will print the variable value of 10, as A a = new B(); explicitly tells a that it is an object of the B class, but we need to access the methods present in the A class. If we want this output as 20, we change the syntax to B a = new B();.

You may get such questions if you attend Java quizzes or a complex interview. These are the important pieces of information that you have to know regarding inheritance, and you can plan accordingly.

Function overloading

Function overloading happens when a class has multiple methods with the same name. If we define a getData method twice in our class, we can say that the getData function is overloaded, as shown in the following code:

```
package coreJava;
//function overloading
public class childlevel extends childClassDemo {

    public void getData(int a)
    {
    }
    public void getData(String a)
    {
    }

    public static void main(String[] args) {
        childlevel cl=new childlevel();
        cl.getData(2);
        cl.getData("hello")
    }
}
```

There are a few rules that we need to remember while using multiple instances of a function with the same name. The first rule is that the number of arguments present in the function-overloaded method should be different, and the second is that the argument data type should be different. If we keep both the getData methods with the int a argument, it will throw an error, so we need to have a different number of arguments for each method. Now, when you print these, you'll get the outputs of 2 and hello. We can see that two different arguments are printed, but with the same method name. Let's add one more getData instance with two arguments, as follows:

```
public void getData(int a, int b)
{
}
```

We now have two instances of getData with the same data type, but the number of arguments varies.

You might come across function overloading in the real world as well, such as when you are asked for the payment method in an e-commerce website in patches. The website might use different getPayment methods to confirm the payment—one getPayment method takes a debit card as an argument, another getPayment method takes a credit card as an argument, and another getPayment might take a gift card as an argument. So we pass different kinds of arguments to the same getPayment method. In this case, we stick to getPayment as a method name and pass it different arguments, bringing the concept of function overloading to this particular scenario.

Function overriding

In this section, let's discuss one more important feature in Java—is function overriding. Let's continue with the same example that we looked at when learning about inheritance.

In that example, we had a parent class called parentClassdemo and a child class called childClassDemo, and the child class inherited the parent class, as follows:

```
package coreJava;
public class childClassDemo extends parentClassdemo {

    public void engine()
    {
        System.out.println("new engine");
    }

    public static void main(String[] args) {
```

```
        childClassDemo cd=new childClassDemo();
        cd.color();
    }
```

Here, we have the `engine` method defined in the child class, which prints a new engine, and we have another method, `color`, which is defined in the parent class, and we call it using an object. If we print this, we will get the output of the `color` method, as it is defined in the parent class. Now, we create a new method in the child class and name it `color` as well, defining it as follows:

```
public void color()
{
    System.out.println("update color");
}
```

We have two instances of the `color` method—one defined in the parent class and a new one defined in the child class. Here is where the concept of function overriding comes into action. If you run the child class, you will get the output of `update color`. This is because the new `color` method defined in the child class overrides the `color` method from the parent class.

This sums up the whole concept of function overriding, where both the methods have the same name, signature, and parameters. In function overloading, we have methods that have the same name, but different arguments. This, one of the major differences between function overloading and function overriding.

Summary

In this chapter, we were introduced to some important Java OOP concepts, such as interfaces, inheritance, function overloading, and function overriding. We looked at each concept using an example, which helped us better understand the concepts in detail.

In the next chapter we will take a look at one of the most important concept in Java code: arrays. We'll see how different arrays look, and how to initialize and display them.

Learn Everything about Arrays

6

In this chapter, we will take a look at one of the most important concept in Java code: arrays. We'll see how different arrays look, and how to initialize and display them. We'll also take a look at a few exercises to help us better understand how arrays work.

We will cover the following topics in this chapter:

- Arrays and their usage in Java programs
- Ways of initializing arrays and assigning objects
- Logic programming on multidimensional arrays
- Practice exercises

Arrays and their usage in Java programs

We might have come across the term array in the past, so let's see what arrays are with an explanation and an example.

An array is a container that stores multiple values of the same data type.

In the following example, we will see what a container is, how to define that container, and how we can store values in them.

If we want to work with arrays, we declare them by allocating some space for them using the following code:

```
int a[] = new int[];
```

The `new` keyword basically allocates memory for a value in this array. The square brackets mean that we are adding multiple values into the brackets, `[]` indicates the term for the array. To define an array, we have to create space for the multiple values that we will be storing in it. In this example, we have five integer values that we are planning to store in the array, which is why we have specified the array data type as an integer, and the number of variables to be added is given in the square brackets:

```
int a[] = new int[5];
```

As we observed in `Chapter 3`, *Handling Strings and Their Functions in Java*, if the values were strings, we would specify the array data type as `String`.

We have declared an array and allocated memory for the values, now we need to pass those values. The first value will be placed in index `0`, the second in index `1`, and so on for all five values. Index naming starts from the `0` index, so the first value will be assigned to the `0` index. This means that we actually initialized values in the array. Now the `a` array holds all the values that we assign to it. For our example, we declare any random values for the array.

Now let's retrieve the values from the array. To do so, we create a `for` loop by typing the following code in the `main` class after declaring the values of the array and leave a print statement after that:

```
for(int i=0; i<a.length;i++);
{
    System.out.println(a[i]);
}
```

Our starting point has been set at index `0` and the limit has been set to the length of the array. Take a look at the `i<a.length` code, `length` is a method that actually returns the size of the array.

On running the code we see that all the values assigned to the array are printed one after the other. In the next section, we will see a simpler way to declare and initialize all the array values.

Ways to initialize arrays and assign objects

In the previous section, we saw how to declare an array; the simplest way is in the form of an array literal. Let's explain this with an example.

We declare another array by typing the following code line in the previous example:

```
int b[] = {1,4,3,5,7,8};
```

What is the difference between the declaration in the previous example and the declaration that we are performing in this example?

In the previous example, we are allocating memory and then assigning the values. In this example, rather than allocating the memory, we are directly passing the values to the array. Here, memory is dynamically allocated, if we add a value in the array declaration, automatically a memory will be allocated and the value will be passed into it. In most cases, coders use this method to declare array values, rather than declaring the allocation and then assigning the values.

Similar to the previous example, the first value is assigned to index 0. If we write a print statement similar to the previous example and run the code, we will see the values of the b array displayed.

That wraps up single-dimensional arrays; let's talk about multidimensional arrays.

Multidimensional arrays

Passing objects in the x axis and y axis is nothing but a multidimensional array. The where the x axis is the row, and the y axis is the column of the matrix in which the array values are given. Multi in this case means we are viewing arrays from the multi-corner perspectives; this is called a **multidimensional** array. The following is a multidimensional array we have created to explain this concept:

```
2   4   5
3   4   7
5   2   1
```

This is a matrix and it has three rows and three columns. 2 is in the zero row and zero column, and the 4 beside it is in the zero row and first column, and the same iteration for the rest of the values. So each argument has an x axis and a y axis.

Let's take an example to explain this. We will create another class, name it Multidimensional.java, and declare a multidimensional array, a, in it:

```
int a[][] = new int[2][3];
```

The first bracket represents the *x* axis or rows, and the second represents the *y* axis or columns. So, the *x* axis takes three values, which means three rows and the *y* axis takes three columns. We then assign the values for each element of the matrix that we created to explain multidimensional arrays. The following code shows how to assign values for the matrix:

```
a[0][0]=2;
a[0][1]=4;
a[0][2]=5;
a[1][0]=3;
a[1][1]=4;
a[1][2]=7;
```

This way we will feed all the values into a multidimensional array. If we want to display the value of the second row, first column, we write a print statement and give the location of the element whose value we wish to display. In this case, we want to display the second row, first column, so the print statement will be written as:

```
System.out.println(a[1][0]);
```

The print statement will display 3, which is the value of the element in that location. In the next section, we will take an example that will help explain how we use all these concepts in solving coding.

How do we print all the values of the a array that we declared in this example? In the earlier example, we printed the array by simply creating a for loop, iterated it from 0 to the length of the array, and the array was displayed.

If we want to declare a multidimensional array in the simplest format, like how array b was described in the previous example, we could write it in the following manner:

```
int b[][]= {{2,4,5},{3,4,7},{5,2,1}};
```

The array will assume that the values in the first bracket are in the zero index, the second in the first index, and the third in the second index. This is the simplest way to declare multidimensional arrays.

Logic programming on multidimensional arrays

Now we will take a look at how we can print all the values of the entire multidimensional array used in the previous section, that is, the a array.

If we analyze the declaration of the array, we will see that two `for` loops will be required to print the entire array, one for rows and one for columns.

We want the controller to scan the complete first row, then the second row, and finally the third. So we add an outer `for` loop for the rows and set the length limit to the number of rows in the array, in this case two rows. The outer `for` loop for the rows will look like the following:

```
for(int i=0;i<2;i++)
```

This `for` loop will actually loop twice since we set the limit to 2 for rows. The first loop will scan the first row and the second loop will scan the second row. Now for each loop, we need to scan the three columns present in that specific row. To do this, we add an inner `for` loop that will scan every column and we set the limit to the number of columns in the array, which is 3 for this example. The inner `for` loop for the columns will look like the following code:

```
for(int j=0;j<3;j++)
```

Finally to print the array, we add a print statement in the internal `for` loop to display all the values. The final code will be as follows:

```
for(int i=0;i<2;i++) //row
{
    for(int j=0;j<3;j++) //coloumn
    {
        System.out.println(a[i][j]);
    }
}
```

Let's try to understand what we have written here. The control will start from the outer `for` loop; this outer `for` loop is executed twice because it has been set to less than 2. After entering the outer `for` loop for the first time, it enters the inner `for` loop; this loop is executed three times because j has been set to less than 3.

Let's debug it and take a look at a few steps in the code to understand these loops better. The following are the steps that will be performed while debugging the code:

1. The controller executes the outer loop for the first time and the value of i has been initialized to 0, this means that the value of the *x* axis is set at 0. The controller will look at the first row since 0 indicates that the first row is being accessed.

2. It moves to the inner `for` loop and executes it, the initial value of `j` has been been initialized to `0`; this means that the value of the *y* axis is set to `0`. The controller will look at the first row and first column, since it was already on the first row because of the outer loop. The inner loop sent the controller to look at the first column.

3. `a` will take the value of the first row and first column as the values of `i` and `j` were initialized to `0`, `a[0][0]`. So the output for this execution will be the first row and first column, which is `2` in this example.

4. The controller moves to the inner `for` loop again as the condition for the loop is still satisfied because `j` gets iterated to `1`, which is less than `3`; this means that the value of the *y* axis is set to `1` and it will access the second column. The controller will look at the first row and second column since it was already on the first row because of the outer loop and the inner loop sent the controller to look at the second column.

5. `a` will take the value of the first row and second column as the values of `i` and `j` are set to `0` and `1`, `a[0][1]`. So the output for this execution will be the first row and second column, `4` in this example.

6. The controller moves to the inner `for` loop again as the condition for the loop is still satisfied because `j` gets iterated to `2`, which is less than `3`. This means that the value of the *y* axis is set to `2` and it will access the third column. The controller will look at the first row and third column since it was already on the first row because of the outer loop and the inner loop sent the controller to look at the third column.

7. `a` will take the value of the first row and third column as the values of `i` and `j` are set to `0` and `2`, `a[0][2]`. So the output for this execution will be the first row and third column, which is `5` in this example.

8. When the controller goes to the inner loop now, it won't be able to execute it because after `j` gets iterated again the value will be `3`, which is not less than the limit we had set for the loop. So the controller exits the inner `for` loop and goes back to the outer loop and iterates the value of `i` to `1`; this means that the value of the *x* axis is set to `1`. The controller will look at the second row since `1` indicates that the second row is being accessed.

9. Steps 2, 3, 4, 5, 6, and 7 are repeated again, but this time the value of `i`, which is the *x* axis, is set to `1`; that means the second row will be accessed. All the values in the second row are displayed according to the steps specified previously, until we reach the third column of the matrix.

10. The controller will exit the inner loop after accessing the third column as j will be iterated to 3, which is less than the limit that we had set for the loop. So the controller again exits the inner `for` loop and starts executing the outer loop.

11. In the outer `for` loop, the value of i will be iterated to 2 and the loop will not be executed because it is not less than 2, which is the limit we set for it.

This is how the values of a multidimensional array can be obtained using two `for` loops, in which the outer loop works with rows and the inner loop works with columns.

Practice exercises

Let's try a few exercises that will help us understand and work with arrays. These exercises will also explain concepts while giving an interview.

Print the smallest number in a 3 x 3 matrix

Let's create another class for this exercise, name it `InterviewMinnumber`, and define the array in the main block. The definition code will be as follows:

```
int abc[][]={{2,4,5},{3,2,7},{1,2,9}};
```

This code declares a 3 x 3 matrix named `abc`. Now we need to traverse each number in the matrix, and look for the smallest number in it. To traverse every number in the multidimensional array, we need to use the same concept that we have used in the *Logic programming on multidimensional arrays* section.

We use two `for` loops here: an outer `for` loop to traverse the rows and an inner `for` loop to traverse the columns. The two `for` loops code will look at follows:

```
for(int i=0;i<3;i++)
    {
    for(int j=0;j<3;j++)
    {
    }
    }
}
```

To find the smallest number, we declare a variable, `min`, and assign the first value of the abc array to it. We assume that the first value in the abc matrix is the lowest value in it.

We add an `if` loop inside the inner `for` loop. Within this `if` loop, whatever we write will go and scan each element in the whole matrix that we declared. In the `if` loop, we add a condition where we check whether the value taken from the matrix at that instance is less than the `min` value. Inside the `if` loop, we swap the value of `min` and `abc`. The final code will be as follows:

```
public class InterviewMinnumber
{
    public static void main(String[] args)
    {
        int abc[][]={{2,4,5},{3,2,10},{1,2,9}};
        int min=abc[0][0];
        for(int i=0;i<3;i++)
        {
            for(int j=0;j<3;j++)
            {
                if(abc[i][j]<min)
                {
                    min=abc[i][j];
                }
            }
        }
        System.out.println(min)
    }
}
```

Let's run the code and see how it finds the smallest number in the matrix.

When the loop is executed first, the value of the first element in the matrix is compared to the value of the `min` variable, but we set the value of the `min` variable equal to the first element, which is 2. We check the condition in the `if` loop, which compares the value of the element in the matrix and the value of `min`. Here, 2 is not smaller than 2, so it does not enter the loop and it goes to the start of the code again. In the next round of the loop, the value of the element changes because we move the next element in the matrix. Now the element being compared is 4, we check the `if` condition again and it won't be true because 4 is not smaller that 2, where 2 is the current value of `min`. Finally, when it reaches the element in the third row first column, 1, then the `if` condition is true and the controller moves inside the loop and assigns 1 to the `min` value. This goes on until the final element in the array matrix, where each value of the `abc` matrix is compared to the value of the `min` variable.

If we debug the code and observe it at every step, we will better understand the logic and working of this code.

Displaying the largest number from the column with the smallest number

In the previous example, we observed how to print the smallest number from the array matrix. In this example, we will look for the smallest number in the matrix and then the maximum number in the same column. The logic behind this is: we first find the minimum number, remember the row number it belongs to, and extract the maximum number in the same column.

Let's use the same matrix that we used in the previous example. The output for this exercise in the matrix that we are using will be 4. The following steps will be implemented to perform this exercise:

1. Find the minimum value in the matrix that we declare
2. Identify the column of that minimum number
3. Find the maximum number in the identified column

We already performed step 1 in the previous example, where we found the minimum number in the matrix, so we will be using the same code for this example and just change the variables a little:

```
int abc[][]={{2, 4, 5}, {3, 0, 7}, {1, 2, 9}}
```

Let's move to step 2. If we observe the code, we see that i stands for the row number and j stands for the column number. So j will take the value of the column where the smallest number is present and we will take this value of j and assign it to a variable that will call mincolumn. So we write code under the swapping command, which will assign the value of j to mincolumn. The code will look something like this:

```
mincoloumn=j;
```

So the moment we find the smallest number in the matrix, we assign to it the value of j, which is the column number to mincloumn. In this case, the value of mincolumn will be 1. This takes care of step 2.

In step 3, we look for the maximum number from the column in which the minimum number is present. We create a `while` loop outside the outer `for` loop that we had created to find the lowest number in the matrix. We initialize the condition variable, k, as 0 and iterate it every time the `while` look condition is met. The condition for the `while` loop is set to k less than 3; this is because we have three rows to traverse to look for the maximum value in them. The code for the `while` loop will look as follows:

```
while(k<3)
{
    k++;
}
```

We declare a variable named `max` and give it an initial value of row 0 and column `mincolumn`. This gives the variable `max` an initial value of 4, since 4 is the first element in the row which contains the minimum number in the matrix. The declaration code will be as follows:

```
int max=abc[0][mincoloumn];
```

Within the `while` loop, we add an `if` loop and set a condition that compares whether the variable in the column with the minimum number is greater than the variable `max` that we declared. If the condition is met, the value of that number is assigned to the `max` variable and the controller moves out of the `if` loop and back to the `while` look after iterating k by 1. The iteration will take the controller to the next row as k is used to signify the row that is being traversed to look for the maximum number.

The code for the `if` loop will look as follows:

```
if(abc[k][mincoloumn]>max)
{
    max=abc[k][mincoloumn];
}
```

So, for the first value of k, which is 0, we go to the first row and second column and assign the value to `max`; in this example, the value is 4. In the `if` condition, we compare the value of the first row, second column with the value of `max`. In this example, both the values are the same, so the `if` loop is not executed and we iterate k and enter the `while` loop again. Next, we compare the value of the second row, second column with the value of `max`; we move to the second row because the value of k is iterated by 1 and the current value of k is 1. So, on comparing, we see that o is less that 4, where 4 is the value of the `max` variable. The condition is not met again and the `if` loop is skipped again. This continues for the third row too and the final value of `max` is 4, which is the largest number in the column. Finally, we leave a print statement to print the value of `max` at the end.

Swapping variables with/without the temp variable

In this exercise, we will be swapping the location of the elements in a simple array and placing them in ascending order.

To do this, we first need to understand the logic of how it will work. Let's take an example to explain this.

We initiate the a array and declare values in it, as shown in the following code:

```
int a[]= {2,6,1,4,9};
```

We can use the bubble-sort mechanism to compare the variables to each other and then place them in the order we want. For the preceding example, the way the logic works will be as follows; we'll compare 2 with 6, 2 with 1, 2 with 4, and 2 with 9. The smallest number after this comparison is 1 and we swap its position with the first index, which is 2. So after swapping, 1 will be the new first index. This means that 1 is the smallest number from the values given in the array. Now we move to the second index, we leave the first index untouched because we have already compared and declared 1 as the fixed first index as it is the smallest number in the array. Now we take the value 6, which is the second index and compare it to other values present in the array. First we compare 6 and 2 and since 2 is smaller than 6 we swap their positions, so 2 is the new first index and 6 is the second index. We then compare 2 with 3; basically we are comparing the first index with all the other values in the array. We then compare 2 to 3, 2 to 4, and 2 to 9; here 2 is the smallest number. So 2 becomes our fixed second index in the array. Now we are left with four values that we need to sort. We again compare 6 with the other values. 6 is smaller than 3, so we swap the positions of 6 and 3. This makes 3 the third index in the array and we compare 3 with the other numbers, 3 is the smallest among all the value given in it. So 3 becomes our fixed third index in the array. Then we perform the same thing for the last three values and conclude that the final arrangement will be 1, 2, 3, 4, 6, 9. Now we need to apply this logic in a Java program and print it.

We will decide on an algorithm for our logic and, based on the algorithm, we will design our code step by step. We will write an outer for loop that moves one index and compares it with the rest.

We write an outer `for` loop and set the condition to not cross the length of the array; here the array size is 5, so the condition is set to i, which is less than 5. If i is 0, the variable value will compare it to the first, second, third, and fourth variables. If i is 2, the variable will compare it to the third and fourth variables. So whatever the i index is, it should start comparing the value of i with its next index. For this, we will create an inner `for` loop and we will initialize the j to be always one number more than i, i plus 1, because we will compare it with the next index. So, if i equals 0, j will be 1. So the zero index will start comparing from the first index. And we compare it until the end of the array, so we set the limit for the inner `for` loop at j, as it's less than the length of the array, which is 5 in this example.

We then add an `if` loop within the inner `for` loop. This loop will do the comparison between the indexes and swap the values when the condition is met. Once the first round of comparisons is done, the controller exits the inner `for` loop and goes back to the outer `for` loop, which is when the smallest number is picked after the comparison, pushed to the corner, and the index moves to the next value.

Now we go back inside the `if` loop and write code to swap the values when the comparison condition is true. To swap variable values, we need to declare a `temp` variable and assign the a[i] number to `temp`. We add the following code to successfully swap the variables:

```
temp=a[i];
 a[i]=a[j];
 a[j]=temp;
```

And in the end, we add a print statement to display the final array after comparing and rearranging the values.

The final output will be displayed as follows:

```
1
2
4
6
9
```

Summary

In this chapter, we covered various concepts in arrays. We took a look at the different types of array, and how they can be initialized and displayed. We then performed different exercises to understand how we can use arrays in different instances.

In the next chapter, we will discuss why the `Date` class and constructors are an important part of Java

7
Understanding Date Class and Constructors in Java 11

The `Date` class and constructors are an important part of Java. In this chapter, we will talk about each of these in detail with the help of some examples.

In this chapter, we will cover:

- The Date class
- The Calendar class
- Constructors
- Parameterized constructors

The Date class

To understand the concept of the `Date` class, we will begin by creating source code for our `dateDemo` class. Let's say we want to print the current date or current time. How do we print that?

At times, we are asked to enter the date into the current date field and we need to get it from Java. In such cases, we will use the Date class, which will give us the current date and current time, in seconds as well. So every detail about the day, week, month, year, or hour can be read through from Java classes. Java has developed a class called Date, from which we can get all these details. The following screenshot displays the source code:

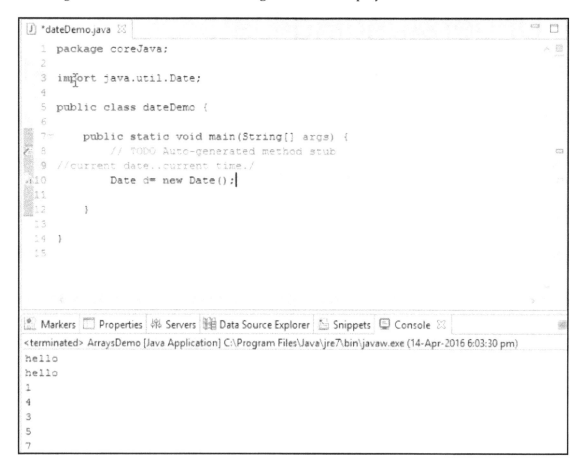

Source code displaying use of date class

Basically, we need to use the methods present in that particular class. To use the methods present in that class, we need to create an object of that particular class. For this, let's consider the following code syntax:

```
Date d= new Date();
```

This `Date` class comes from the `util` package, and `d` is the object of the `Date` class where date and time are present. In the previous chapter, we saw that Java has some packages, such as the `java.lang` package which traps all fundamental Java stuff, and `java.util`, which is where we have collection framework and the `Date` class.

The preceding code syntax says that we do not know where the `Date` class is. To make this class available to our Java file, we need to import the `util` Java package because this `Date` class is packed into that particular package. If we use it to import the package into the preceding class, you can use that date successfully. Move your mouse here and it says `import 'Date' (java.util)`, as shown in the following screenshot:

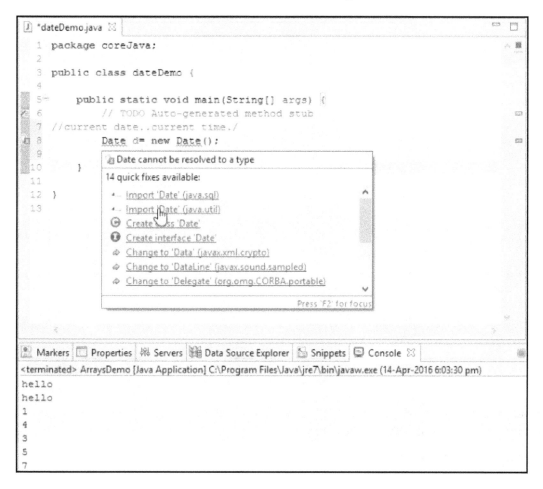

Quick fixes drop down with suggestions to correct the code error

Once you click on that, you will see:

```
import java.util.Date
```

Where `util` is the package, and `Date` is a class.

As we have seen, `d` is the object that contains the date and time, but how do we print it? Because it is an object format, we cannot simply use the following:

```
System.out.println(d)
```

To convert it into readable text, refer to the following screenshot:

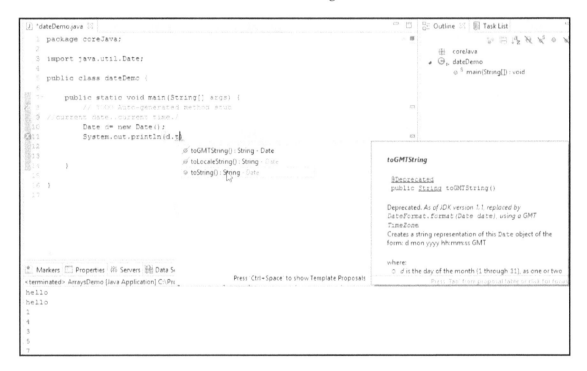

Converting the code into readable text format

Here, we are converting `Date` into a string so that we can visually see it in our output. On running the preceding code as shown in the screenshot, it prints the following:

```
Fri Apr 15 17:37:27 EDT 2016
```

This is how we can print the entire date, time, and month from our current system's Java date. The format in the preceding output is not what we generally get, but it might be in a specific format, such as:

```
mm//dd//yyyy
```

If we want to extract our date in the preceding format, how do we do that?

The d object gives us all the details. But how can we convert all these details into the preceding format? For this we will use the following:

```
Date d= new Date();

SimpleDateFormat sdf=new SimpleDateFormat("M/d/yyyy");
System.out.println(sdf.format(d));
System.out.println(d.toString());
```

The output of the preceding code syntax will be:

Output displaying date and time as per the code

Refer the following URL for the `SimpleDateFormat` format code:

- `http://www.tutorialspoint.com/java/java_date_time.htm`

Now, on altering the object and the `SimpleDateFormat` code, we see the following:

```
Date d= new Date();

    SimpleDateFormat sdf=new SimpleDateFormat("M/d/yyyy");
    SimpleDateFormat sdf=new SimpleDateFormat("M/d/yyyy hh:mm:ss");
    System.out.println(sdf.format(d));
    System.out.println(sd.toString());
    System.out.println(d.toString());
```

The output will be:

Output displaying the date and time in a new format

Thus, we can actually format our date as per our requirements and pass that into the `SimpleDateFormat` method. We can bring the d object and place it into an argument so that it will be formatted in a particular manner. This is how dates are retrieved using Java.

In the next section, we will see how to use the `Calendar` class.

The Calendar class

In the previous section, we explored the `Date` class, where we learned about `Date` methods and how to operate on them using simple date format standards. In this section, we will learn about the `Calendar` class, which is similar to the `Date` class, but with some extra features. Let's see what they are and how we can use them to extract our date formats using the `Calendar` class.

First, we will create a class with a different name to avoid conflict. To create a `Calendar` instance, run the following:

```
Calendar cal=Calendar.getInstance();
Date d=new Date();
```

The steps are similar to those for the `Date` class. However, the `Calendar` object has some unique features that date doesn't support. Let's explore them.

Use the following code snippet:

```
Calendar cal=Calendar.getInstance();
SimpleDateFormat sd=new SimpleDateFormat("M/d/yyyy hh:mm:ss");
System.out.println(sd.format(cal.getTime()));
```

The output for the preceding code will be:

```
J dateDemo.java    J calendarDemo.java ⊠
  1  package coreJava;
  2
  3  import java.text.SimpleDateFormat;
  4  import java.util.Calendar;
  5
  6  public class calendarDemo {
  7
  8      public static void main(String[] args) {
  9          // TODO Auto-generated method stub
 10
 11          Calendar cal=Calendar.getInstance();
 12          SimpleDateFormat sd=new SimpleDateFormat("M/d/yyyy hh:mm:ss");
 13          System.out.println( sd.format(cal.getTime()));
 14
 15
 16      }
 17
 18  }
 19
```

```
 Markers    Properties   Servers   Data Source Explorer   Snippets   Console ⊠
<terminated> calendarDemo [Java Application] C:\Program Files\Java\jre7\bin\javaw.exe (15-Apr-2016 5:56:29 pm)
4/15/2016 05:56:29
```

Output displaying date and time using calendar class

Now, suppose we want to print the day of the month and week too. We will add the following line of code to the preceding snippet:

```
System.out.println(cal.get(Calendar.DAY_OF_MONTH));
System.out.println(cal.get(Calendar.DAY_OF_WEEK_IN_MONTH));
```

The output will be as follows:

```
dateDemo.java    calendarDemo.java ⌧
  1  package coreJava;
  2
  3  import java.text.SimpleDateFormat;
  4  import java.util.Calendar;
  5
  6  public class calendarDemo {
  7
  8      public static void main(String[] args) {
  9          // TODO Auto-generated method stub
 10
 11          Calendar cal=Calendar.getInstance();
 12          SimpleDateFormat sd=new SimpleDateFormat("M/d/yyyy hh:mm:ss");
 13          System.out.println( sd.format(cal.getTime()));
 14          System.out.println(cal.get(Calendar.DAY_OF_MONTH));
 15          System.out.println(cal.get(Calendar.DAY_OF_WEEK_IN_MONTH));
 16
 17      }
 18
 19  }
 20
```

```
Markers   Properties   Servers   Data Source Explorer   Snippets   Console ⌧
<terminated> calendarDemo [Java Application] C:\Program Files\Java\jre7\bin\javaw.exe (15-Apr-2016 5:58:29 pm)
4/15/2016 05:58:30
15
3
```

Output displaying date, time, day of the month and day of week in month using calendar class

Similarly, we can see from the following screenshot that there are multiple properties to choose from:

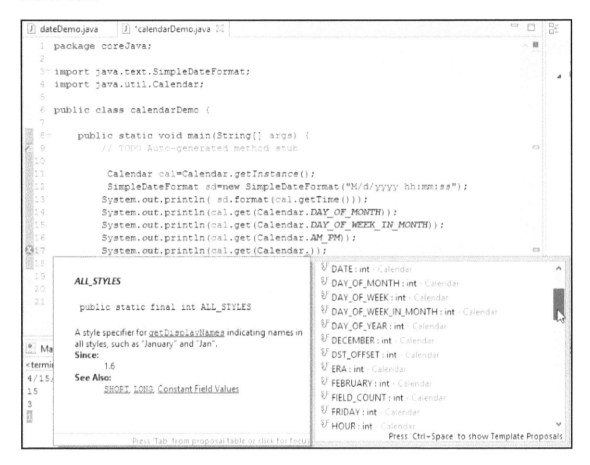

Drop down displaying multiple properties for the calendar class

Thus, here we have used the `Calendar` instance to actually get the system date and time, but in the previous class we used `Date` instance; that's the only difference. A lot of methods are present in this `Calendar` instance that you will not find in the `Date` class.

This is how the system date can be retrieved as per our requirements.

Constructors

The constructor is one of the most important concepts in the Java programming language. Thus, before we see an example, let's understand what a constructor is.

A constructor executes a block of code whenever an object is created. That means that, whenever we create an object for the class, automatically a block of code will get executed. In other words, a constructor is invoked whenever an object is created.

So where is a constructor used and how do we define it? A constructor should be written, it's just like a method, but the only difference between a method and a constructor is that a constructor will not return any values, and the name of the constructor should always be a class name.

To create a constructor for this class, we will write the following code syntax:

```
public class constructDemo()
{
//
}
```

From the preceding code syntax, it is evident that whatever is written in this constructor will be executed whoever creates an object and calls the constructor. If we create an object for the preceding class called `constructorDemo`, automatically the set of lines present in this block will get executed. That's the main aim of the constructor:

```
package coreJava;

public class constructDemo {
    public constructDemo()
    {
        System.out.println("I am in the constructor");
    }
    public-void getdata()
    {
        System.out.println("I am the method");
    }
    // will not return value
    //name of constructor should be the class name
    public static void main(String[] args)  {
        // TODO Auto-generated method stub
        constructDemo cd= new constructDemo();
```

Whenever the preceding line is executed, the control will automatically check whether there is an explicitly-defined constructor. If it is defined, it will execute the particular block. Whenever one creates an object, a constructor is called in Java.

The output of the preceding code will be:

```
I am in the constructor
```

We are not actually creating a constructor for every class but we are specifically bringing in the constructor concept now as, earlier, we did not use any concept when we defined the constructor. Now if we use this command, the program will still run, but this time it will not execute that block. If we do not define any constructor, the compiler will call the default constructor. We might call it an implicit constructor.

We mostly depend on constructors in real-time to initiate objects, or define variables for our program. The constructor and normal methods look similar as they define the access modifier in brackets, but will not accept any return type, but in this case it accepts. Thus, if we write:

```
public constructDemo()
{
    System.out.println("I am in the constructor");
    System.out.println("I am in the constructor lecture 1");
}
```

The output for the preceding code will be:

```
I am in the constructor
I am in the constructor lecture 1
```

Therefore, in general, people use the preceding code block to define variables or initiate properties in real-time, and they go ahead with using the constructor.

In the next section, we will look at another constructor that we have in Java.

Parameterized constructors

The constructor we learned about in the previous section is the default constructor because it does not accept any values. In a parametric constructor with the same syntax, we actually come up with some parameters, as shown in the following screenshot:

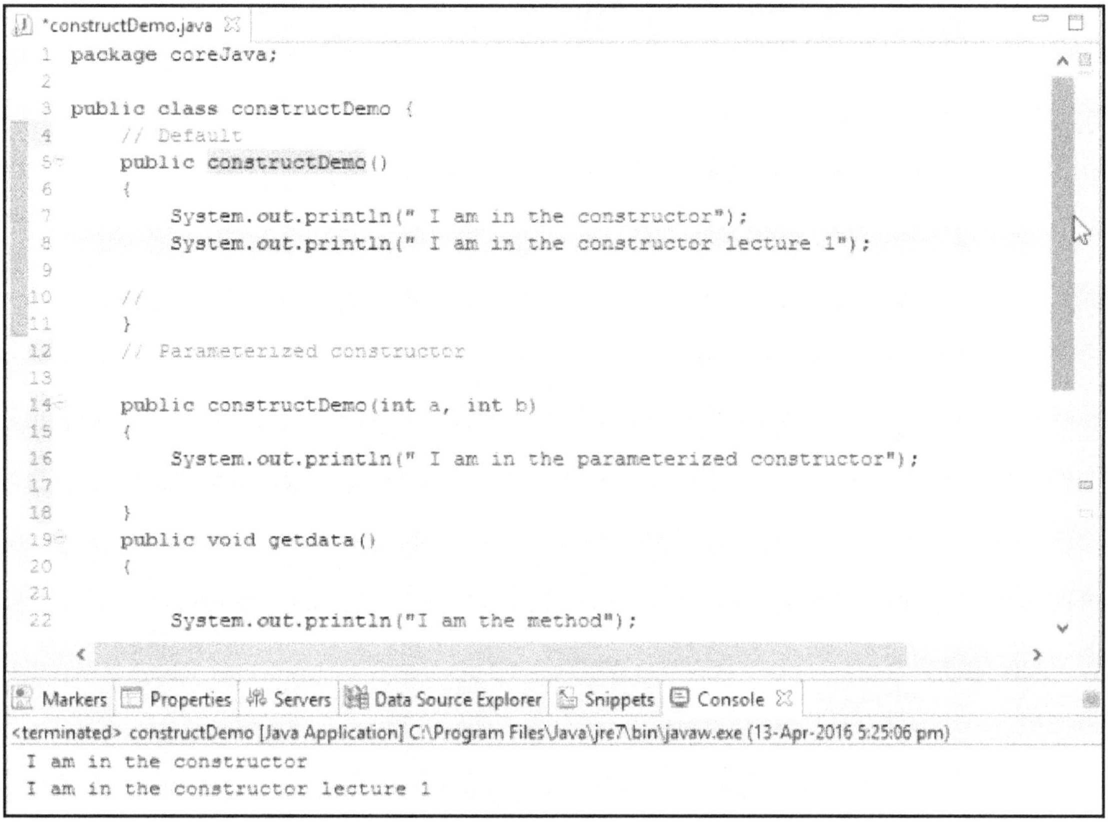

```java
1  package coreJava;
2
3  public class constructDemo {
4      // Default
5      public constructDemo()
6      {
7          System.out.println(" I am in the constructor");
8          System.out.println(" I am in the constructor lecture 1");
9
10         //
11     }
12     // Parameterized constructor
13
14     public constructDemo(int a, int b)
15     {
16         System.out.println(" I am in the parameterized constructor");
17
18     }
19     public void getdata()
20     {
21
22         System.out.println("I am the method");
```

Markers Properties Servers Data Source Explorer Snippets Console

<terminated> constructDemo [Java Application] C:\Program Files\Java\jre7\bin\javaw.exe (13-Apr-2016 5:25:06 pm)

```
I am in the constructor
I am in the constructor lecture 1
```

Output for the parameterized constructor using the given code

The only difference between the previous constructor and this one is that here we are passing the parameters, and in the default one pass it without any parameters. When we run our code, whenever we create an object, if we don't pass any parameters, the compiler automatically picks the default constructor, as shown in the following screenshot:

```
constructDemo.java

19       public void getdata()
20       {
21
22           System.out.println("I am the method");
23       }
24
25       //will not return values
26       //name of constructor should be the class name
27
28       public static void main(String[] args) {
29           // TODO Auto-generated method stub
30
31           //constructDemo cd= new constructDemo();
32           constructDemo c= new constructDemo(4,5);
33
34           // compiler will call implict constructor if you have not defined const
35           //when ever you create an object constructor is called
36       //block of code when ever an object is created
37       }
38
39 }
```

Markers ☐ Properties 🔍 Servers 🔲 Data Source Explorer 📄 Snippets 🖥 Console ⊠
<terminated> constructDemo [Java Application] C:\Program Files\Java\jre7\bin\javaw.exe (13-Apr-2016 5:29:00 pm)
I am in the parameterized constructor

Output when the default parameter is passed

Now, let's create one more object for the same class with parameters:

```
constructDemo c=new constructDemo(4,5);
```

When we define parameters as mentioned in the preceding syntax, the compiler checks whether there is any constructor with the two arguments of the integer type while executing the runtime. If it finds a constructor, it executes the following code syntax instead:

```
public constructDemo(int a, int b)
{
```

```
        System.out.println("I am in the parameterized constructor");
    }
```

In cases where a parameter is not defined, the compiler executes the default constructor. The output for the preceding code will be:

I am in the parameterized constructor

At runtime, when creating an object, we have to give the parameters, so during execution, it will compare the parameters with the constructors defined. Similarly, we can create multiple objects for the same class:

```
constructDemo cd=new constructDemo();
constructDemo c=new constructDemo(4,5);
```

When both the constructors are run together, the output will be:

I am in the constructor
I am in the constructor lecture 1
I am in the parameterized constructor

Now, we will create one more constructor of a similar type, but this time with only one parameter:

```
public constructDemo(String str)
{
    System.out.println(str);
}
public static void main(String[] args)
{
    constructDemo cd=new constructDemo("hello");
}
```

The output will be:

hello

Thus, the Java compiler gives preference to the explicit constructor if we define something explicitly, otherwise it prints the implicit constructor. The key points to be noted here are that it will not return any value and the constructor has to be defined with the class name only.

Summary

In this chapter, we ran a few examples of code to understand how the `Date` class, the `Calendar` class, and the constructors work.

In this chapter we will take a look at three keywords: `super`, `this` and discuss the `finally` block.

8
Importance of the super and this Keywords and Exceptions in Java

In this chapter, we will take a look at two keywords: `super` and `this`. We will pick examples and explain how they are put to use in various situations while writing our Java code. We will also take a look at exceptions and how we can use them to handle situations where the code fails due to some error. We'll wrap up the chapter with a section on the `finally` block.

In this chapter, we will cover the following topics:

- The super keyword
- Practical usage of the super keyword
- Importance of the this keyword
- Different kinds of exceptions
- The try...catch mechanism to handle exceptions
- Importance of the finally block in Java

The super keyword

In general, when people inherit properties from a different class, there might be a redundancy if the same variable names are used in both the parent and child class. To differentiate between parent variables and child variables, we use the `super` keyword.

Let's explain this using an example. Let's create two classes and name them `childDemo` and `parentDemo`. In the `parentDemo` class, we define a string called `name` and assign the `'rahul'` string to it.

Now, in the `childDemo` class, we inherit the properties of `parentDemo`. We know how to inherit the properties of a parent class using the `extends` keyword, which we learned in `Chapter 5`, *Everything You Need to Know About Interfaces and Inheritance*. The code to inherit the properties is given here:

```
public class childDemo extend parentDemo{
```

In this code, `childDemo` is taking the properties of `parentDemo`.

Add a string in the `childDemo` class, call it `name`, and assign the `QAClickAcademy` string to it. We then define a method called `public void getStringdata()` inside the `childDemo` class and give a statement to print the value of `name` as the output. We define another method, called `public static void main(String[] args)`, outside `getStringdata()` and create an object for the child class, `childDemo cd = new childDemo();`. Once the object is created, we add another line of code below it: `cd.getStringdata();`. This calls the `getrStringdata()` method, so obviously the name is printed as the output, which is `QAClickAcademy`. Even though we are inheriting the properties of the `parentDemo` class, which also contains a string with the same name, the print statement calls the value of string in `childDemo`. This is because Java gives preference to the local variable.

Whenever there is a collision between the variable names of the parent and the child, it gives preference to the local variable, in this case the `childDemo` class. What if we are working on a project where we need to print the string name in the `parentDemo` class as well? For this, we use the `super` keyword to refer to the `parentDemo` class, from which we inherit the properties to the `childDemo` class. So, if we want to call the name variable from the `parentDemo` class, we add a print statement and add a `super` keyword before the variable we want to print—this will get the value from `parentDemo`. When we run the code now, we get both the parent object and the child object as an output as we have left a print statement for the name string in both classes. The code for the `parentDemo` class is given as follows:

```
public class parentDemo{
    String name= "Rahul";
    public static viod main (String[] args){
    }
}
```

The code for the `childDemo` class is given as follows:

```
public class childDemo extends parentDemo{

    String name = "QAClickAcademy";
    public void getStringdata();
    {
        System.out.println(name);
        System.out.println(super.name);
    }

    public static void main(String[] args){
    childDemo cd = new childDemo();
    cd.getStringdata();
    }
}
```

The final output will be:

```
QAClickAcademy
Rahul
```

Practical usage of the super keyword

In this section, we will take a look at the different ways to use the `super` keyword in Java.

Using the super keyword for methods

We saw how to handle the parent variable with the help of the `super` keyword. In this section, we will see how to handle two methods if their names are the same in the `parentDemo` and `childDemo` classes. We'll use the previous example in this section too.

In the `parentDemo` class, add a method called `getData()`, and inside the method give a print statement to display the "I am in parent class" message. If we want to execute the `getData()` method in the `childDemo` class, we write `cd.getData()` in the `main` method of the `childDemo` class. We can access `getData()` as we are inheriting the properties of the `parentDemo` class. If we run the `childDemo` class, we will receive the previous example's output as well as the new sentence we added in the `parentDemo` class, I am in parent class.

In the `childDemo` class, we will define another method with the same name as that of the `parentDemo` class and add a print statement to display the I am in child class message. If we run the `childDemo` class, we will get the previous example's output and then I am in child class is displayed. This is because preference is given to the local class, so the `getData()` method in the `childDemo` class overrides the `getData()` method in the `parentDemo` class.

Now, we want to use the `getData()` method of the `parentDemo` class in the `childDemo` class. To do this, we simply do what we did for variables: add `super.getData()` inside the `getData()` method of the `childDemo` class. When we run the `childDemo()` class, we get the previous example's output followed by I am in parent class and then I am in child class.

Using the super keyword for constructors

Let's use the `super` keyword for constructors in this section. We'll use the previous example here too.

In the `parentDemo` class, we define a constructor, `parentDemo()`, and add a print statement to print: Parent class constructor.

In `childDemo`, we define a constructor `childDemo()` and add a print statement to print: Child class constructor. If we want to use the `parentDemo` class constructor in the `childDemo` class, we add the `super()` method in the `childDemo()` constructor. This makes the controller invoke the constructor in the `parentDemo` class.

There's an important rule we need to follow when working with constructors: whenever you use a `super` constructor in a child constructor, it should always be the first line in it.

When we run the `childDemo` class, the controller first executes the `super()` method. It goes to the `parentDemo()` constructor and executes it and then `childDemo()`. So the final output will be:

```
Parent class constructor
Child class constructor
QAClickAcademy
Rahul
I am parent class
I am in child class
```

Importance of the this keyword

There is one more keyword in Java that is just like the super keyword: this. In this section, we will take a look at the this keyword.

Let's explain the this keyword with an example. Create a class named thisDemo and declare a variable, a, and assign the value 2 to it. We define a getData() method in its class, declare the a variable inside it, and assign the value 3 to it. We also add a print statement in it. The code will look as follows:

```
package coreJava;public class thisDemo
{
    int a= 2;
    public void getData()
    {
        int a= 3;
        System.out.println(a);
    }
}
```

As we can see, the value of a is 2 in the entire class, but in one specific method, getData(), we want the value of the variable to be 3. In this code, we want to call both values of a, that is, 2 and 3. We create an object in the main method and add the td object in it. The code for the td object is as follows:

```
thisDemo td=new thisDemo();
td.getData();
```

If we run the code, the output we get is 3. But we want to print the value of a as 2 in the same block too. This is when the this keyword comes into play. The scope of the class object will be at the class level and not the method level. So we say that the getData() method refers to the current object and the object scope lies in the class level. So a= 2 is valid for the entire class, and a=3 is valid just for the getData() method. This is why we call the a variable in the getData() method, a local variable, and and the a variable in the class, a global variable.

To print the global variable of the example that we are working on, we need to add a print statement in the getData() method and we add this.a in the print statement. The print statement will look as follows:

```
System.out.println(this.a);
```

When we run the code, we get the following output:

```
3
2
```

This wraps up our example on the this variable. Now let's learn about exceptions.

Different kinds of exception

In this section, we will take a look at how we can handle exceptions in Java.

In general, if there is an error in the code, we need to catch it and print a message without failing; this can be done using the `try...catch` mechanism. So in general, when we try to write code and we suspect that there might be an error in it, we will use that error for exception handling.

We'll explain it with the help of an exercise. Let's create a new class, `exceptionDemo`, and inside the `main` block we declare the a, b, and c variables and assign values of 4, 7, and 0, respectively, to them. We add a `try` block inside the main block and we declare an integer variable, k, which is equal to b divided by c. Whenever we add anything in the `try` block, we are trying to see whether the code works. If it fails, the controller will come out of this `try` block and enter into the `catch` block that contains the exception. An important point to remember is that the `catch` block comes right after the `try` block. Inside the `catch` block, we write a print message to display `I caught the error/exception`.

When the controller goes into the k variable line, the script fails because `7/0` is infinity, which is an arithmetic exception but the script will not fail immediately. If we don't write the `try...catch` block, we see a different kind of error.

Let's take out the `try...catch` block, run the code, and see the error we get. We see an error in the output section, `Java.lang.ArithmeticException`; this is because we cannot divide 7 by 0, so the script fails abruptly.

If we initially feel that we will get an error in our code, we can simply make a script to pass and catch the error by putting a proper debug message that can be handled with the help of the `try...catch` mechanism. Now, let's add the `try...catch` blocks again and debug the entire code. The output will be `I caught the error/exception`; this is because 7 divided by 0 is infinity so here the script should fail, but we did not see any error in the output section saying the code has failed. This is because the controller simply moves to the `catch` block and executes it. The final code will look as follows:

```
public static void main(String[] args)
{
    int b=7;
    int c=0;
    try
```

```
    {
        int k=b/c;
        System.out.println(k);
    }
    catch(Exception e)
    {
        System.out.println("I caught the error/exception")
    }
}
```

The output will be as follows:

```
I caught the error/exception
```

The try...catch mechanism to handle exceptions

In this section, we will use one `try` followed by multiple `catch` blocks. There are different types of exceptions in Java, and for each exception we can add separate `catch` blocks.

Let's explain this using the previous example. The exception written for the previous code is a general exception, so for any error in the `try` block, the general exception is executed. Now let's try and catch a specific exception. We can add a `catch` block under the `try` block, and add a specific exception and a print statement to print, `I caught the Arithmeticerror/exception`. The code for the specific catch block is:

```
catch(arithmeticException et)
{
    System.out.println("I caught the Arithmeticerror/exception");
}
```

When we run the code, we get the following output:

```
I caught the Arithmeticerror/exception
```

We see that, when we ran the code, the controller went to the `catch` block, because the `catch` block is specifically written for an arithmetic exception, and the error thrown also belongs to arithmetic errors. So once the controller receives an error, the `try` block will see which kind of `catch` block is related to it and run it.

There are many other exceptions in Java: we can just Google and take a look at them.

Importance of the finally block in Java

There is one more block that is just like the `try...catch` block: is the `finally` block. The `finally` block will be executed irrespective of whether an exception is thrown. This block is executed if the program runs successfully, and even executed if the program doesn't run.

We'll explain this using the example we used in the *The try...catch mechanism to handle exceptions* section. We just add a `finally` block after the `catch` blocks and we give a print statement in it saying, `delete cookies`. The code block will look like this:

```
finally
{
    System.out.println("delete cookie")
}
```

When we run the code, we get the following output:

```
I caught the Arithmeticerror/exception
delete cookie
```

One important point is that `finally` can work with or without the `catch` block; all it needs is to be written below a `try` block.

Summary

In this chapter, we took a look at the `super` and `this` keywords. We also looked at examples to explain where we can use these keywords to overcome certain obstacles. We learned about exceptions, and implemented them in various instances where the code failed due to an error. We also learned about the `finally` block.

In the next chapter, we will dive deep into the collections framework, which consists of interfaces and classes. We will also take a look at the three major collections: `List`, `Set` and `Map`.

Understanding the Collections Framework

9

In this chapter, we will delve into the collections framework, which consists of interfaces and classes. We will have a look at the three major collections: `List`, `Set`, and `Map`. `ArrayList` from the `List` collection, `HashSet` from the `Set` collection, and `HashMap` and `HashTable` from the `Map` collection will be discussed in this chapter. We will go through each concept by looking at examples.

We will cover the following topics in this chapter:

- The collections framework
- The list collection
- The set collection
- The map collection

The collections framework

The Java collections framework is basically a collection of interfaces and classes. To program efficiently, or use the flexibility of Java methods, Java has designed a framework, which consists of different classes and interfaces. The collections framework helps in storing and processing data efficiently. This framework has several useful classes that have tons of useful functions, that make a programmer's task super easy.

We have seen a lot of concepts about arrays and multidimensional arrays. For example, in an array, if we want to delete one of the indexes out of a new set of arrays, we can do that using the collections framework. Let's say in one array there are 10 values, and we want to remove the fifth value, or insert a value between the fifth and sixth values—there are some flexibility methods that you will get in the collections framework.

The kinds of method available in this collection framework, and how they can be used effectively, will be discussed in further sections. So just to give you an idea, remember that a collection is a set of classes and interfaces.

We will have a look at the collections this framework has to offer.

The List collection

The first one is the `List` collection/interface. A list is an ordered collection, sometimes we call it as a sequence as well. Lists may contain duplicate elements, just like arrays, but there are lots of differences between an array and `ArrayList`. You can insert multiple values into this `List` container, and it might contain duplicate elements as well. You can actually add any value and remove any value from any index. Let's say you added 15 elements sequentially into the list, now you want to remove 6th element, or you want to insert an element between the 10th and 11th elements, or you want to know an element at what index it is out of those 15 elements. There are lots of helpful APIs to retrieve elements from the list container, which we don't get in arrays. Arrays can only be initialized; apart from that, you cannot perform any methods on an array, whereas with `ArrayList` you have lots of flexible methods to play around with.

The `List` interface is a collection, and `ArrayList`, `LinkedList`, and `vector` are the three classes that implement this interface. This interface provides a set of methods. It exposes a few methods, whereas these three classes use these methods in their classes.

Out of these three, let's discuss `ArrayList`. This is one of the most famous ones, and is used by most Java programmers. Once you understand `ArrayList`, you can easily figure out `LinkedLists` and `vector`. In the next section, we will create an `ArrayList` class and implement methods present in the `List` interface, to see how flexible these methods are at retrieving or organizing data. When you have a set of data in a container, you can easily organize that data with the help of the `List` interface.

The ArrayList class

Let's get started with the `ArrayList` class, which implements the `List` interface. Create a new class and name it `arrayListexample`. We will first look at the methods present in `ArrayList`, and then we'll discuss the difference between an array and `ArrayList`.

We start by declaring `ArrayList` as follows. If you hover over `ArrayList` in your IDE, you'll see a suggestion telling you to import `java.util` for `ArrayList`:

```
package coreJava;

public class arrayListexample {

    public static void main(String[] args) {

        ArrayList a=new ArrayList();

    }
}
```

Once you do this, it'll still show a suggestion for `ArrayList`, and if you hover over it, it will suggest adding argument types. To remove this suggestion, you can pass an argument type to `ArrayList`, such as `Integer` or `String`:

```
ArrayList<String> a=new ArrayList<String>();
a.add("rahul");
a.add("java");
```

After passing the argument type, you can easily add some string instances by using `a.` and it'll show you a list of different types supported by `ArrayList`. For `ArrayList`, we didn't define a specific array size, whereas when you see in arrays, we have explicitly defined a size. In arrays, once we define the size, you cannot decrease or increase the size. But in `ArrayList`, you could add or delete elements anytime from the list, it is a dynamic size array. This is one of the basic differences between array and `ArrayList`.

If we want to print this `ArrayList`, we can simply do that by adding the following line of code:

```
System.out.println(a);
```

On running, it prints `[rahul, java]`. But if you want to print this in arrays, we need to write a `for` loop. We add another object and this time we specify the index where we want the string to go:

```
a.add("rahul");
a.add("java");
System.out.println(a);
a.add(0, "student");
System.out.println(a);
```

When we print this, it gives the following output:

```
[rahul, java]
[student, rahul, java]
```

You can see that in the second line, `student` is added before `rahul` in the list as we have specified its index as `0`.

If we want to remove an entry from the list, we can do that by adding the following lines of code:

```
a.remove(1);
a.remove("java");
```

The first line of code will remove the entry from the list present at the first index, whereas the second line will find the string in the list and remove it. If you want to get the entry for a specific index, you can do that using the `get` method:

```
a.get(2);
```

The preceding line of code will print `java` as the output, as it is the element present at index `2`.

Let's say you have a list of 50 elements, and you need to find out whether a particular string/integer is present in that list. If you were to go with arrays, you would have to create a `for` loop and find out whether the element is present, but in `ArrayList`, we have a `contains` method that checks the entire list for us and gives the output in the form of `true` or `false`:

```
System.out.println(a.contains("java"));
```

This will print the output as `true` as the element is present in our list; if you change it to, for example, `testing`, it will return the value as `false` as it is not present in our list.

Another useful method present in `ArrayList` is the `indexOf` method. If we want to find the index value of a particular element from the list, we can know that by using `indexOf`:

```
System.out.println(a.indexOf("rahul"))
```

This will return the index number of this string.

Now, if we want to check whether the array is empty, we can do that using the `isEmpty` method in `ArrayList`, which will return the value as `true` or `false`:

```
System.out.println(a.isEmpty());
```

This will return the value as `false` as our list is not empty.

The last and most important method in `ArrayList` is the `size` method, which returns the length of the list:

```
System.out.println(a.size());
```

 One more thing you need to know about `ArrayList` is that all the classes that implement the `List` interface can accept duplicate values. We know the classes that extend `List` in the collection interface: `ArrayList`, `LinkedList`, and `vector`. And all these classes can accept duplicate values.

Example of ArrayList

Let's say we have an array with duplicate numbers, such as {4, 5, 5, 5, 4, 6, 6, 9, 4}, and we want to print out the unique number from this, and how many times this number is repeated in this array. Our output should be "four is repeated three times, five is repeated three times, six twice, nine once."

Let's bring in the `ArrayList` concept here to solve this puzzle:

```
package demopack;
import java.util.ArrayList;
public class collectiondemo {
    public static void main(String[] args) {
        int a[] ={ 4,5,5,5,4,6,6,9,4};
        ArrayList<Integer>ab =new ArrayList<Integer>();
        for(int i=0;i<a.length;i++)
        {
            int k=0;
            if(!ab.contains(a[i]))
            {
                ab.add(a[i]);
                k++;
                for(int j=i+1;j<a.length;j++)
                {
                    if(a[i]==a[j])
                    {
                        k++;
                    }
                }
                System.out.println(a[i]);
                System.out.println(k);
                if(k==1)
                    System.out.println(a[i]+"is unique number");
```

```
            }
          }
        }
      }
```

The preceding snippet is the entire code required to solve this puzzle. Let's try to understand the key logical concepts within the code. We start by defining the array and then create an empty `ArrayList` with the ab object type. Then we create a `for` loop, and within it we use an `if` loop with `!ab.contains` to check whether the element is present within the loop. We need another `for` loop within this `if` loop to iterate through the remaining part of the array. The `if` loop within this `for` loop will work as a counter for us to increment the number of times a number is repeated in the array.

We're done with the `for` and `if` loops. We print out each element from the array and the number of instances each element is present in the array. To print the unique number, that is, the number that is not repeated in the array, we use an `if` loop and print it.

That's it for this example; you can try coding this example with your own logic.

The Set collection

Another important collection present in Java is the `Set` collection/interface. `HashSet`, `TreeSet`, and `LinkedHashSet` are the three classes that implement the `Set` interface. The main difference between `Set` and `List` is that `Set` does not accept duplicate values. One more difference between the `Set` and `List` interfaces is that there is no guarantee that elements are stored in sequential order.

We will mainly be discussing `HashSet` in this section. We will take an example class and try to understand this concept. Create a class and name it `hashSetexample` for this section, and create an object within the class to use `HashSet`; it'll suggest you add the argument type, which is `String` in our case:

```
package coreJava;

import java.util.HashSet;

public class hashSetexample {

    public static void main(String[] args) {
        HashSet<String> hs= new HashSet<String>();

    }
}
```

In your IDE when you type `hs .`, it'll show you all the methods provided by `HashSet`:

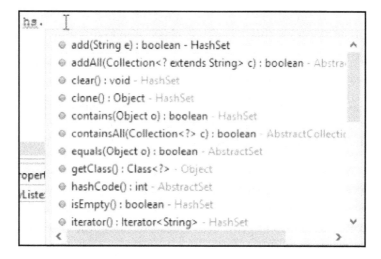

Start by adding a few string instances of duplicate entries:

```
HashSet<String hs= new HashSet<String>();
hs.add("USA");
hs.add("UK");
hs.add("INDIA");
hs.add("INDIA");
System.out.println(hs);
```

When you print this, the output will be as follows:

```
[USA, UK, INDIA]
```

We see that the duplicate entry for `INDIA` is rejected by `HashSet` and we only see one instance.

If we wish to remove any object, we can do so using the `remove` method, and to get the size of the list use the `size` method:

```
System.out.println(hs.remove("UK"));
System.out.println(hs.isEmpty());
System.out.println(hs.size());
```

The `isEmpty` method tells us whether the list is empty—if it's empty, it'll return `true`, otherwise it returns `false`.

Using iterator

To iterate through each element present within a list, we use the `iterator` method. We need to create another object for this `Iterator` class, along with the `String` argument type:

```
Iterator<String> i=hs.iterator();
```

Imagine that we have a set of elements and they are in order starting from zero, one, two, and so on. `iterator` goes through each element starting from zero and prints the element present at each value. We have created an object for iterator and we print the values as follows:

```
System.out.println(i.next());
System.out.println(i.next());
```

The first instance of `i.next()` will print the values present at the zero index and the next `i.next()` instance prints the value at index one. If we have a set where we have around 100 values, we will have to use the `while` loop:

```
while(i.hasNext())
{
    System.out.println(i.next());
}
```

Here, we have used the `hasNext` method, which checks the set for next values. If there are values present in the next index, it'll return `true` and if not, it returns `false`. In our case, it'll return `true` for 100 values and `false` after that, and exit the `while` loop.

This is how you can iterate through the objects present in the `Set` interface using `iterator`. If you are working on automation testing, such as Selenium, you'll be using this `while` loop frequently.

The Map collection

We have one more collection, called `Map`. We will take an example and discuss `Map` as we proceed with the code. This interface takes the values in the form of a key and value pair.

We create a class, `hashMapexample`, and within that the we define `HashMap`. `HashMap` requires two types of argument, such as `Integer` and `String`:

```
package coreJava;

import java.util.HashMap;

public class hashMapexample {

    public static void main(String[] args) {
        HashMap<Integer, String> hm= new HashSet<Integer, String>();

    }
}
```

Here, `Integer` is the key and `String` is the value. Now if you type `hm.` in your IDE, you will see a few methods present in `HashMap`; let's use the `put` method:

```
hm.put(0,  "hello");
hm.put(1,  "goodbye");
hm.put(2,  "morning");
hm.put(3,  "evening");
```

The `put` method takes the input in the form of keys and values. Also, the value of the key needs to be an integer, it can be a string as well. The key is just something we define for the value. We can remove a value using the `remove` method:

```
hm.remove(2);
```

The `entrySet` method in `HashMap` stores each key and value in the form of a set index:

```
Set sn= hm.entrySet();
```

We have now converted this `HashMap` into a set. To traverse through each index of this set, we use `iterator` and, just like in the previous section, we use the `while` loop:

```
Iterator it= sn.iterator();
while(it.hasNext())
{
    Map.Entry mp=(Map.Entry)it.next();
    System.out.println(mp.getKey());
    System.out.println(mp.getValues());
}
```

We need to use `Map.Entry` here, as the element in each index consists of a key and a value, and `Map.Entry` helps us to separate out the keys and values. When you print this `while` loop, you should get the following output:

```
0
hello
1
goodbye
2
morning
3
evening
```

Without using `Map.Entry`, it'll throw an error. This is how `HashMap` works.

HashTable

There is one more collection, called `HashTable`, but it lies along the same lines as `HashMap`. You just need to change `HashMap` to `HashTable`—that's it. There's a slight difference between `HashMap` and `HashTable` though.

The differences between `HashMap` and `HashTable` are as follows:

- Synchronized or thread-safe
- Null keys and null values
- Iterating values

Synchronized or thread-safe

This is the most important difference between the two. `HashMap` is non-synchronized and not thread-safe. So what is meant by non-synchronized? It means if multiple programs simultaneously access `HashMap`, it keeps on updating. Now let's say there are five threads working on `HashMap`. That means five different programs or threads can access `HashMap` at the same time, which means there is no synchronization. But in `HashTable`, if one program is accessing `HashTable`, the other program needs to wait until the first program releases the `HashTable` resources. That's the major difference. On the other hand, `HashTable` is thread-safe and synchronized. When should you use `HashMap`? If your application does not require a multithreading task—in other words, `HashMap` is better for non-threading applications. `HashTable` should be used in multithreading applications.

Null keys and null values

HashMap allows one null key and any number of null values, while HashTable does not allow null keys and null values in the HashTable object. Let's say you are entering employee records into a database and while uploading the employee details into your database, maybe you feel that you would not know their phone number, but you enter the field called phone number in a key value, and index value for now you would leave it as a null; you could update it later. This works in HashMap, but when you are working with HashTable, it will not allow any null keys and null values. If you feel that you want to make your program very secure and you want to block multiple threads from accessing it simultaneously, then you should go with HashTable. HashTable is thread-safe, and it will not release its object to another program until one program completes its operation on HashTable.

Iterating values

HashMap object values are iterated by using iterator. HashTable is the only class other than vector which uses enumerator to iterate the values of the HashTable object.

The operations are the same across HashMap and HashTable, except for the three differences we've just described.

Summary

In this chapter, we had a look at the collections framework and the three types of collection: List, Set, and Map. We explored ArrayList in the List collection, and also explored an example of ArrayList. The Set collection is different from ArrayList—the major difference is that Set does not accept duplicate values. In the last collection, that is, the Map collection, we saw two types, HashMap and HashTable, and the differences between the two.

10
The Importance of the final Keyword, Packages, and Modifiers

This is the final chapter in our book. Here, we will be dealing with some more important concepts that will help us write and execute better code.

In this chapter, we will look at the following concepts:

- The final keyword
- Packages
- Modifiers in Java

The final keyword

First, we will create a new class. If we declare any variable as `final`, that means the value cannot be changed again. Let's consider the following code:

```
package coreJava;

public class finaldemo {

    public static void main(String[] args) {
        //TODO Auto-generated method stub
        final int i=4; //constant variables
    }
}
```

As you can see, we have declared the integer value as 4. This means we cannot change this value to another number. If we try to do that, it throws an error saying `Remove 'final' modifier of 'i'`. This keyword is useful if we want a value to be constant.

If we mark a class as `final`, it will throw an error because when we change the access mode to `final`, we are not able to use that as a parent class. In other words, we will not be able to inherit our properties from it. If we want to inherit our properties, we need to change it back to `public`. The key logic for the final keyword is that, once written, we cannot override `final` methods. So these are unique and cannot be used again with the same name.

The `final` keyword can be used at the method level to make sure that the method is not overridden. It is used at the variable level to make sure we're not changing it, and it can also be used at the class level to ensure that we are not inheriting that parent class.

But remember not to confuse `final` and `finally`. `finally` is something that is related to `try...catch` exceptions. Once you execute the `try` or `catch` block, and preface any error, the controller will still come to this log and execute the code, no matter whether the script is pass or fail. `finally` is all about restricting access, such as we cannot use that, inherit that, or even change the values. We have explored packages, and how to import packages into other classes. We have explored the inheritance of interfaces, runtime polymorphism, strings, and many more. This is all about keywords.

In the next section, we will learn about packages.

Packages

When scripts are written for each Java class, there is a pre-populated line that is present automatically. It is `package coreJava`. Since we have created a package in Java and placed all the Java classes into that `coreJava` package, we see it as `package coreJava`.

Packages are nothing but a set of classes and interfaces. For example, Java comes with a few built-in packages, such as `java.length`; if we import this package, only then can we access a basic fundamental method, such as `public static void main`, integer, or array. All these classes come from this `java.lang` package. It is important to define the package name, because without it, we cannot access the classes present inside the package. This is because `java.lang` is a default package and it comes within the Java compiler itself.

We have another package as well, `java.util`. We used this package when we worked on collections; we imported a `java.util` package. In order to work on `ArrayList`, this class is present in the `java.util` package. Therefore, if we remove `import java.util.ArrayList`, it throws an error because it does not belong to `java.lang`. All collection interfaces come from the `util` package.

But how do we know what keyword to use? The following screenshot displays what Eclipse will display if we hover the mouse:

Quick fixes drop down with suggestions to correct the code error

We are importing the `java.util` package. And from that package, we are importing the `ArrayList` class. The syntax for it will be:

```
import package.classname
```

Here, the reason why we are using `ArrayList` in this Java class is because we know that `ArrayList` is in the `java.util` package. But we need not remember it when we are working with Eclipse. When you just hover the mouse, it suggests we import the package and we can just click on it. It will automatically import that particular test.

`HashSet` imports the `HashSet` class from the same `util` package. If we go to `HashMap`, it brings `HashMap`. Thus, whenever we want to work on some tests, we need to import that package or class. `System.out.println()` also comes from one package only, but they come from `java.lang`, which is a built-in compiler. These are inbuilt inside the Java packages.

At the same time, we can also define a user-defined Java package. In this case, all our test cases are in a different package called `coreJava`. If someone wants to use our classes, all they need to do is run `import coreJava.classname`.

In the next section, we will look at the public modifier.

Modifiers in Java

There are four types of access modifiers:

- `public`
- `private`
- `protected`
- `default`

We will not discuss the theory here as you can find it on Google. We need a practical approach as to where exactly these access modifiers are used, or where exactly the packages are imported. Whenever we've created a method throughout this book, every time we just used `public` and wrote the method. The three other access modifiers work similarly.

Now let's try to understand how each of these access modifiers can help us.

default

If we do not mention any access modifier, our Java class automatically thinks it has a `default` access modifier. If it is `default`, that means you can access this method anywhere in your package. But if you go out of this package, then you cannot access this method. Even if we import the `package.classname` into our new package, we will not be able to access this method if we have not specified it as `public`. If you don't specify it, then by default it thinks it's a `default` access modifier. The `default` access modifier can be accessed anywhere in the package, but not outside it.

In the *Packages* section, we imported this package and we tried to use it. As you can see in the following screenshot, there is an error showing up in line **15**:

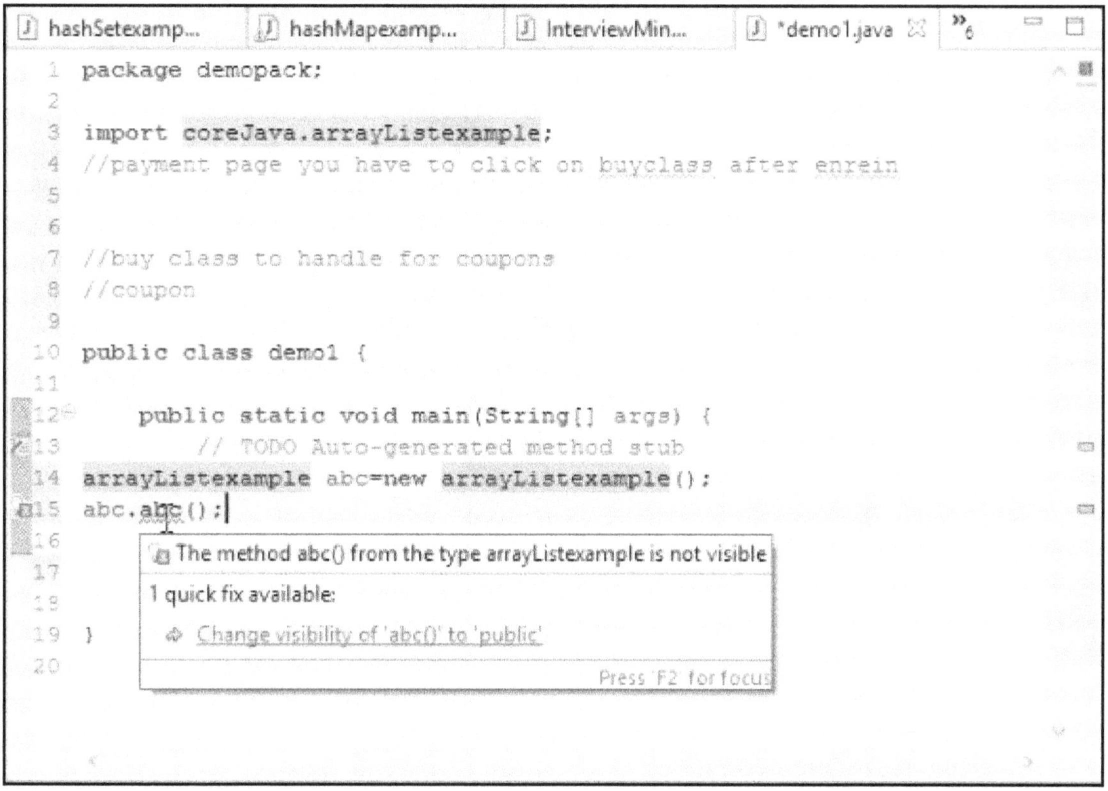

Quick fixes drop down with suggestions to correct the code error for default

If we don't specify anything, we cannot access it, therefore it is the same as that of the default feature. This applies to variables as well:

```
public class arrayListexample {
    // can accept duplicate values
    //ArrayList, LinkedList, vector- Implementing List interface
    //array has fixed size where arraylist can grow dynamically
    //you can access and insert any value in any index
    int i=5;
```

As we can see, in the preceding code we have declared an integer. However, it will not be `public`; it is `default`. Thus, we cannot access the variable outside the package. If we import it, we will have access to the class but not the methods. If we want access, we have to write it as a `public`. So what does a `public` access modifier do?

public

On making the method or variable `public`, we will have access to it across all the packages. That means basically everywhere. There is no restriction for this package of this class. The error observed in the preceding screenshot is also goes once we make the method/variable `public`.

The following screenshot displays the `int` value after we made it `public`:

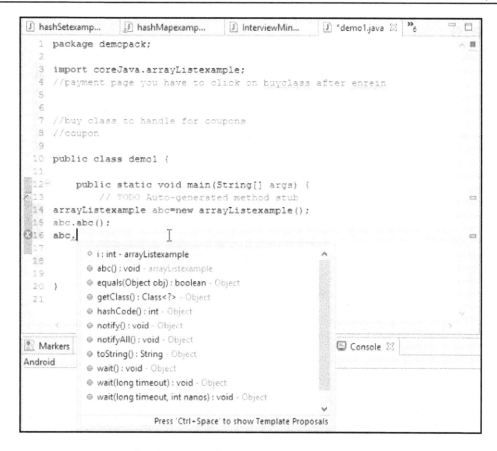

Quick fixes drop down with suggestions to correct the code error for public

In the next class, we'll look at what `private` and `protected` access modifiers are. There are two more access modifiers after this one, let's see what they do.

private

If we mark our method or variable as private, then we cannot access either of them outside the class. They cannot be accessed outside the package, or outside the same class. If we want to access this in our ArraysDemo example, we cannot do that. Even if we try to, it throws an error, as shown in the following screenshot:

Quick fixes drop down with a suggestion to correct the code error for private

This is so because, if we mark any method or variable as private, we cannot access it outside that particular class. Until and unless we change it to something else, it throws an error. This applies to the variable as well.

If you want a real-time scenario, let's say you are making a payment and buying a product; all the credit card details will go as private because they will not be accessed outside of that buy class. If they can be accessed, that's a security breach, right? So to make credit card details restricted to that particular class, the developers give the private variable to all the card details so other classes cannot use it. Even if they have used inheritance or are importing a package, they will not have access to those sensitive details. There are a lot of real-time scenarios; if you are working on test frameworks, there might be some variables which you should not change, and always keep it private.

protected

If we define a variable or method as `private`, we can access them in subclasses only. This means if we define it as `protected`; then, whichever class is inheriting the parent class, only those subclasses can have access to the method, and no other classes. This can be understood with the following code snippet:

```
protected void abc() {
    //TODO Auto-generated method stub
    System.out.println("Hello");
    }
```

The difference between `default` and `protected` is that in `default` we can access a class only within the same package of classes. Even `protected` can access all classes in the same package, except it has an additional feature. This additional feature says that, if we want to access it in other packages, only subclasses that inherit the properties of the parent class can access it.

The same concept is applied to variables.

Summary

In this chapter, we learned concepts that help us understand the importance of packages, modifiers, and the `final` keyword in Java.

I hope you have a better understanding of these concepts now that you've read all the chapters.

Other Books You May Enjoy

If you enjoyed this book, you may be interested in these other books by Packt:

Selenium Framework Design in Data-Driven Testing
Carl Cocchiaro

ISBN: 978-1-78847-357-6

- Design the Selenium Driver Class for local, remote, and third party grid support
- Build Page Object Classes using the Selenium Page Object Model
- Develop Data-Driven Test Classes using the TestNG framework
- Encapsulate Data using the JSON Protocol
- Build a Selenium Grid for RemoteWebDriver Testing
- Construct Utility Classes for use in Synchronization, File I/O, Reporting and Test Listener Classes
- Run the sample framework and see the benefits of a live data-driven framework in real-time

Test-Driven Java Development - Second Edition
Alex Garcia, Viktor Farcic

ISBN: 978-1-78883-611-1

- Explore the tools and frameworks required for effective TDD development
- Perform the Red-Green-Refactor process efficiently, the pillar around which all other TDD procedures are based
- Master effective unit testing in isolation from the rest of your code
- Design simple and easily maintainable code by implementing different techniques
- Use mocking frameworks and techniques to easily write and quickly execute tests
- Develop an application to implement behavior-driven development in conjunction with unit testing
- Enable and disable features using feature toggles

Leave a review - let other readers know what you think

Please share your thoughts on this book with others by leaving a review on the site that you bought it from. If you purchased the book from Amazon, please leave us an honest review on this book's Amazon page. This is vital so that other potential readers can see and use your unbiased opinion to make purchasing decisions, we can understand what our customers think about our products, and our authors can see your feedback on the title that they have worked with Packt to create. It will only take a few minutes of your time, but is valuable to other potential customers, our authors, and Packt. Thank you!

Index

about 6
access modifiers 134
editor tools, working with 15, 16, 20, 21
executable program, writing 22, 27, 29
finally block 118
installation 6, 9, 11, 14

L

List collection
  about 120
  ArrayList class 120
  ArrayList, example 123

M

Map collection
  about 126
  HashTable 128
methods
  accessing, in different class 40
  using 33, 36
multidimensional arrays
  about 83
  logic programming 84

N

nested loops
  about 66
  examples 68

O

object-oriented programming systems (OOPS) 5
object
  accessing, in Java 38
  assigning 82
  creating, in Java 37
  in Java 36

P

packages 132
parameterized constructors 107, 109

S

Set collection
  about 124
  iterator, using 126
String class
  about 46
  methods 46, 49
  object, creating 44
String literal
  defining 44
strings
  about 43
  and variables, differentiating 32
  logic, reversing 49
super keyword
  about 111
  using 113
  using, for constructors 114
  using, for methods 113

T

this keyword
  importance 115
traffic light system
  interfaces, using with 72, 75
try...catch mechanism
  using, for handling exceptions 117

V

variables
  swapping, with/without the temp variable 91

W

while loop
  about 61
  do...while loop 65

www.ingramcontent.com/pod-product-compliance
Lightning Source LLC
Chambersburg PA
CBHW080534060326
40690CB00022B/5130